# PRESSURE COOKER RECIPES

Easy, Quick & Healthy Recipes for Lowcarb & Paleo Diet

(Delicious and Healthy Recipes for Deeply Satisfying Meals)

**Richard Elliott**

Published by Sharon Lohan

© **Richard Elliott**

All Rights Reserved

*Pressure Cooker Recipes: Easy, Quick & Healthy Recipes for Lowcarb & Paleo Diet (Delicious and Healthy Recipes for Deeply Satisfying Meals)*

ISBN 978-1-990334-23-8

All rights reserved. No part of this guide may be reproduced in any form without permission in writing from the publisher except in the case of brief quotations embodied in critical articles or reviews.

Legal & Disclaimer

The information contained in this book is not designed to replace or take the place of any form of medicine or professional medical advice. The information in this book has been provided for educational and entertainment purposes only.

The information contained in this book has been compiled from sources deemed reliable, and it is accurate to the best of the Author's knowledge; however, the Author cannot guarantee its accuracy and validity and cannot be held liable for any errors or omissions. Changes are periodically made to this book. You must consult your doctor or get professional medical advice before using any of the suggested remedies, techniques, or information in this book.

# Table of contents

Part 1 .................................................................................. 1

Introduction .......................................................................... 2

Chapter 1: Pressure Cooker Soup And Stew Recipes ...................... 3

Pressure Cooker Chile Con Carne ............................................. 3

Chickpea Soup ...................................................................... 5

Barley Soup .......................................................................... 7

Tomato Basil Soup ................................................................. 9

Vegetable Chicken Soup ........................................................ 10

Creamy Cauliflower Soup ....................................................... 11

Lentil Spinach Soup .............................................................. 13

Green Chile Chicken Chili ...................................................... 15

Potato And Bean Soup .......................................................... 17

Spicy Chicken Soup .............................................................. 18

Squash Soup ........................................................................ 20

Tomato Chicken Rice Soup .................................................... 21

Ham and Bean Stew .............................................................. 23

Mediterranean Turkey Soup ................................................... 23

Chapter 2: Pressure Cooker Main Dish Recipes ......................... 26

Creamy Pressure Cooker Mushroom Chicken ........................... 26

Easy Pressure Cooker Butter Chicken ..................................... 29

Beef Short Ribs .................................................................... 31

Honey Mustard Pork Chops ................................................... 33

Chunky Beef Stew ................................................................. 35

| | |
|---|---|
| Teriyaki Chicken | 37 |
| Juicy Pressure Cooker Pot Roast | 38 |
| Lemon Salmon | 39 |
| Garlic Honey Chicken | 41 |
| Lime Chicken Thighs | 42 |
| Pressure Cooker Tips: | 44 |
| 1-Lemon Marinated Tuna | 45 |
| 2-Pressure Cooker Carrot Soup with Cream | 47 |
| 3-Chicken Curry with Tomato | 49 |
| 4-Quick Pressure Cooker Brown Rice | 51 |
| 5-Pressure Cooker Pasta with Cheese | 53 |
| 6-Portabella Risotto | 55 |
| 7-Simple Lentil Soup | 57 |
| 8-Pressure Cooker Spicy Chickpeas Curry | 59 |
| 9-Mashed Potatoes | 61 |
| 10-Pressure Cooker Tomato Basil Soup | 63 |
| 11-Pressure Cooker Lemon Chicken with Cheese | 65 |
| 12-Pressure cooker Strawberry Jam | 67 |
| 13-Pressure Cooker Split Peas | 69 |
| 14-Pressure Cooker Rice with Peas | 71 |
| 15-Pressure Cooker BBQ Sauce | 73 |
| 16-Quick Beef Stew | 75 |
| 17-Pressure Cooker BBQ Chicken | 77 |
| 18-Pressure Cooker Apple Sauce | 79 |
| 19-Pressure Cooker Mix Fruit Risotto | 81 |
| 20-Rice Pudding with Blueberries | 83 |

21-Pressure Cooker Sweet Potatoes ................................................. 85

22-Pressure Cooker Roasted Potatoes ............................................... 87

23-Pressure Cooker Lentils with Spinach ........................................... 89

24-Pressure Cooker Kidney Beans Stew .............................................. 91

25-Pressure Cooker Healthy Oatmeal ................................................ 93

26-Simple Healthy Yellow Rice ..................................................... 95

27-Pressure Cooker Potato and Onion Soup .......................................... 97

28-Pressure Cooker Quick Pork ..................................................... 99

29-Pressure Cooker Roasted Turkey Legs ............................................ 101

30-Pressure Cooker Chicken Stock .................................................. 103

31-Pressure Cooker Chicken Stew ................................................... 105

32-Pressure Cooker BBQ Ribs ....................................................... 107

33-Pressure Cooker Mashed Turnip .................................................. 109

34-Pressure Cooker Carrot Puree ................................................... 111

35-Pressure Cooker Shrimp Rice .................................................... 113

36-Pressure Cooker Vegetable Broth ................................................ 115

37-Pressure Cooker Mushroom Broth ................................................. 117

38-Pressure Cooker Fish Stock ..................................................... 119

39-Yellow Split Pea and Red Lentil Soup ........................................... 121

40-Pressure Cooker Mango Jam ...................................................... 123

Part 2 ............................................................................ 125

Introduction ...................................................................... 126

Pressure Cooker Recipes ........................................................... 133

Rice 'N Tips ...................................................................... 135

Barbecue Ribs ..................................................................... 136

Cheesy Mushrooms and Rice ......................................................... 138

| | |
|---|---|
| Chicken and Sausage Delight | 139 |
| Chicken Noodles | 141 |
| Chicken and Salad | 142 |
| Jambalaya | 144 |
| Pintos and Ham | 146 |
| Pork Chops with Potatoes and Carrots | 148 |
| Seasoned Cabbage | 149 |
| Spicy Rice Pilaf | 150 |
| Split Pea Soup | 152 |
| Tender Chicken and Vegetables | 154 |
| Blissful Beef Stew | 156 |
| Pleasantly Pleasing Pork Ribs | 158 |
| Mexicana Tamale Surprise | 160 |
| Sensational Steamed Salmon | 162 |
| Favorite Veggies and Chicken Stew | 164 |
| Creamy Fresh Tomato Soup | 166 |
| Wholesome Lentil Soup with Ham | 168 |
| Flavorful Homemade Tomato Sauce with Fettuccine | 170 |
| Tender & Tasty Chicken and Rice | 172 |
| Quick & Easy Pressure Cooker Chili | 174 |
| Tilapia with Basil Tomato Sauce | 176 |
| Seasonal Vegetable Stew | 177 |
| Too Good to Miss Chicken N Dumplings | 178 |
| So Simple Vegetarian Baked Beans | 180 |
| Scrumptious Sweet Potatoes and Pork | 181 |
| Spur of the Moment Swiss Steak | 183 |

Queen of Crab ................................................................................. 184

Lobster Sea Mania ........................................................................ 186

Frozen Paste Chicken ................................................................... 188

Conclusion ..................................................................................... 190

# Part 1

# Introduction

For the women of today who has to play various roles – homemaker, mother, career person, hostess – the pressure cooker is one of the most valued possessions. It allows her to make delicious meals for the family and for parties in very less time than it takes to prepare regular food. Lesser cooking time means that the retained natural flavors, minerals and vitamins. Generally the cooking is done in the pressure cooker, so there is less mess to clear up.

Pressure cooking is a way of cooking food in sealed pan using liquid, pan to retain steam and build pressure inside. By increasing the pressure in the pan, the boiling point of liquid in the pressure cooker is increased to 115°C to 120°C, significantly higher than the normal boiling point of 100°C. The heighten temperature of the water and steam causes the fibers of the food to crack down more rapidly, and shortens the cooking time by up to 75 percent.

This book covers a range of non-vegetarian and vegetarian recipes – from starters and soups to great desserts. All of them carefully explained and clearly illustrated. Enjoy these delightful recipes and share them with your friends and family.

# Chapter 1: Pressure Cooker Soup And Stew Recipes

## Pressure Cooker Chile Con Carne

Ingredients
1 (2 1/2-pound) bottom round roast, trimmed and cut into 1-inch cubes
3/4 teaspoon salt, divided
2 medium onions, chopped
2 (6-inch) corn tortillas
4 teaspoons olive oil, divided
6 garlic cloves, minced
3 tablespoons chili powder
2 tablespoons ground ancho chile pepper
1 tablespoon ground cumin
3 tablespoons unsalted tomato paste
1 tablespoon finely chopped chipotle chile, canned in adobo sauce
1 teaspoon dried oregano
1 teaspoon lower-sodium soy sauce
1/4 teaspoon ground cinnamon
2 (14.5-ounce) cans unsalted fire-roasted diced tomatoes

1/2 ounce semisweet chocolate, chopped
Chopped green onions (optional)
1 sliced radish
1 tablespoon ground cumin

Directions

Place tortillas in the bowl of a food processor; process to form fine crumbs.

Heat a 6-quart pressure cooker over medium-high heat. Add 1 teaspoon oil to pan; swirl to coat. Sprinkle beef with 1/2 teaspoon salt. Add one-third of beef to pan; sauté 3 minutes or until browned on all sides. Remove beef from pan. Repeat procedure twice more with 1 teaspoon oil and one-third of beef.

Add remaining oil to pan; swirl to coat. Add onion and garlic; sauté 3 minutes. Add tortilla crumbs, chili powder, and next 8 ingredients; stir well. Stir in beef.

Close lid securely; bring to high pressure over high heat. Adjust heat to medium-high or level needed to maintain high pressure; cook 25 minutes. Remove from heat; let stand 20 minutes.

Place cooker under cold running water to release pressure. Remove lid; stir in chocolate and remaining salt, stirring until chocolate melts.

Top with green onions and radish, if desired.

# Chickpea Soup

Ingredients
1 tablespoon olive oil
1 1/2 cups chopped onion
5 garlic cloves, minced
4 ounces Spanish chorizo, diced
2 1/2 cups water
2 1/2 cups fat-free, lower-sodium chicken broth
1 1/2 cups dried chickpeas (garbanzo beans)
2 bay leaves
6 cups chopped escarole
1 tablespoon sherry vinegar
3/8 teaspoon kosher salt
1/2 teaspoon freshly ground black pepper
1/4 teaspoon crushed red pepper

Directions
Heat a 6-quart pressure cooker over medium-high heat. Add oil to pan; swirl to coat. Add onion; sauté 3 minutes.

Add garlic and chorizo; sauté 2 minutes.
Stir in 2 1/2 cups water, broth, chickpeas, and bay leaves. Close lid securely; bring to high pressure over high heat.
Adjust heat to medium or level needed to maintain high pressure; cook 1 hour.

Remove from heat; release pressure through steam vent, or place cooker under cold running water to release pressure. Remove lid. Discard bay leaves.

Add escarole and remaining ingredients, stirring just until escarole wilts. Serve immediately.

# Barley Soup

Ingredients
1 cup lentils, rinsed
2 stalks celery, sliced
½ cup hulled barley or ½ cup pearl barley
½ teaspoon oregano
6 cups water or 6 cups vegetable stock
½ teaspoon ground cumin
1 onion, chopped
¼ teaspoon black pepper
2 garlic cloves, minced or crushed
⅛-¼ teaspoon red pepper flakes
2 carrots, sliced
½ teaspoon salt (optional)
2 -4 cups fresh spinach (optional)

Directions
Put all ingredients except salt and spinach into cooker and bring it to high pressure.
Cook at high pressure for 12 minutes; then bring pressure down with a quick-release method. Lentils should be cooked, but barley may not be completely tender.
Cook until barley reaches the desired state of tenderness, about 15 minutes, adding water if a thinner consistency is needed. Then add salt and spinach, if desired.

Cook briefly until spinach is wilted but still bright green.

# Tomato Basil Soup

Ingredients
2 (14.5 oz) cans chicken broth
3 lbs tomatoes – cored, peeled, and quartered
1/4 cup fresh basil
1 tablespoon tomato paste
1/2 teaspoon salt
1/2 teaspoon freshly ground black pepper
1/2 cup shredded Parmesan cheese
1 cup half and half
3 tablespoons butter
1 large onion, diced
2 stalks celery, diced
1 large carrot, diced
2 garlic cloves, minced or pressed

Directions
Melt butter in pressure cooker pot. Saute onions, celery, and carrots until tender. Add garlic and cook 1 minute stirring often. Add chicken stock, tomatoes, basil, tomato paste, salt, and pepper.
Select high pressure and 5 minutes cook time. When timer sounds turn pressure cooker off, wait 5 minutes and use Quick Pressure Release to release pressure.
When valve drops carefully remove lid. Puree mixture until it's very smooth.
Saute and stir in Parmesan and half and half.

# Vegetable Chicken Soup

Ingredients
1 1/2 lbs boneless skinless chicken breasts
1 onion, coarsely chopped
1 cup carrot, peeled and cut in 1 inch chunks
1 cup celery, cut in 1 inch chunks
1/4 cup cilantro, chopped
1/2 cup green onion, chopped
3 garlic cloves, chopped
1 1/2 teaspoons salt
1/2 teaspoon black pepper
4 cups water
1 1/2 cups corn kernels, frozen

Directions
Cut chicken breasts into 1 inch cubes. Place chicken, onion, carrots, celery, cilantro, green onion, garlic, salt, pepper and water in pressure cooker.
Lock lid into place. Over high heat, bring cooker up to pressure. Then reduce heat to maintain pressure and pressure regulator rocks gently. Cook for 8 minutes.
Quickly release the pressure. Carefully remove lid and add frozen corn.
Heat on medium heat until corn is tender.

# Creamy Cauliflower Soup

Ingredients
1 tablespoon coconut oil
1 white onion
3 cloves garlic
1 extra large or 2 medium sized fennel bulbs, stalks and fronds removed
1 pound cauliflower florets
1 cup coconut milk
3 cups broth (bone broth or vegetable broth)
2 teaspoons salt
Optional: Truffle oil, for serving
Optional: Black pepper for serving

Directions

Slice the onions, mince the garlic, and chop the fennel. If your cauliflower is not already chopped into florets, do that now.

In the bottom of your pressure cooker, heat up the coconut oil. Sauté the onions until translucent.
Add the garlic, fennel, and cauliflower. Sauté for 5-10 minutes, until the edges of the vegetables begin to turn golden.
Pour the broth and coconut milk into the pot. Add salt. Cook on the soup setting for at least 5 minutes.

Once the pressure cooker is done cooking, release the pressure and remove the lid.

Use a standing blender or an immersion blender to puree the soup to a smooth, creamy consistency.

Scoop into serving bowls and drizzle with truffle oil. Top with freshly cracker pepper, and garnish with a left over fennel frond. Serve hot.

# Lentil Spinach Soup

Ingredients
4 cups chicken broth
4 cups water
1 1/2 cups brown lentils, rinsed
2 teaspoons cumin
1 teaspoon garlic salt
1/4 teaspoon red pepper flakes
2 tablespoons dried parsley
1/2 teaspoon salt
1/2 teaspoon pepper
1/2 cup orzo
2 cups roughly chopped baby spinach
1 tablespoon vegetable oil
1 onion, diced
3 carrots, diced
5 cloves garlic, minced
2 cans (15 oz.) diced tomatoes

Directions
Select sauté and add oil to cooking pot. When oil is hot, sauté onion and carrots until tender, about 8 minutes. Add garlic, cook for one minute. Add tomatoes, broth, water, lentils, cumin, garlic salt, red pepper flakes, parsley, salt and pepper.

Select high pressure and 10 minutes cook time. When beep sounds turn pressure cooker off, use a Quick Pressure Release to release the pressure.

When valve drops carefully remove lid, tilting away from you to allow steam to disperse.

Select Simmer and add orzo; simmer 10 minutes or until orzo and lentils are tender.

Add spinach and cook until spinach wilts.

Season to taste with additional salt and pepper if necessary.

# Green Chile Chicken Chili

Ingredients
2 cans (14 ounce) chicken broth
1 jar (16 ounce) salsa verde
1 can (4 ounces) diced green chilies
1 teaspoon cumin
1/4 teaspoon red pepper flakes
2 cans (15.5 ounce) cannellini beans or other white bean, drained and rinsed
2 tablespoon cornstarch
3 tablespoon cold water
1 tablespoon vegetable oil
1 large onion, diced
2 cloves garlic, minced or pressed
3 cups cooked, diced or shredded chicken

Directions
Select Sauté and add the oil to the pressure cooker pot. When oil is hot, add the onion and cook, stirring occasionally until the onion is tender, about 5 minutes. Add the garlic and cook for an additional minute.

Add chicken, chicken broth, salsa verde, green chilies, cumin, red pepper flakes and beans to the pressure cooking pot. Lock lid in place, select High Pressure, 5 minutes cook time and press start.

When timer beeps, turn off pressure cooker, wait 5 minutes, then do a quick pressure release to release any remaining pressure.

In a small bowl, dissolve cornstarch in 3 tablespoons water. Select Simmer and add cornstarch mixture to the pot stirring constantly until chili thickens. Add salt and pepper to taste.

Served topped with sour cream, diced avocado, tortilla chips, and shredded cheese.

# Potato And Bean Soup

Ingredients
2 lb potatoes, peeled and cut into chunks
1 lb leeks, trimmed and sliced into thin pieces
1 can cannellini beans, drained and rinsed
Marigold Swiss Bouillon Powder, as needed

Directions
Cook the potatoes in the pressure cooker with water to cover until just tender. Drain the cooking water into a bowl.
Reserve some of the potato pieces to add texture to the soup.
Measure the cooking water and make up the stock according to the guidelines on the carton. Puree the remaining potato and add the stock to it.
Meanwhile steam the leeks until cooked and add to the soup with the cooking liquid then add the beans and the reserved potato chunks.
Add freshly ground black pepper to taste. Serve hot with crusty bread.

# Spicy Chicken Soup

Ingredients
2 (14.5 ounce) cans chicken broth
1/2 teaspoon salt
1 teaspoon ground black pepper
1 teaspoon garlic powder
2 tablespoons dried parsley
1 tablespoon onion powder
1 tablespoon chili powder
2 (16 ounce) cans black beans, drained
1 (15 ounce) bag frozen corn
2 tablespoons olive oil
1 large onion, diced
3 cloves garlic, minced or pressed
4 boneless, skinless chicken breasts
1 (16 ounce) jar mild chunky salsa
2 (14.5 ounce) cans peeled and diced tomatoes

Directions
Select Sauté and add olive oil to the pressure cooker pot. When oil is hot, add the onion and cook, stirring occasionally until the onion is tender, about 5 minutes. Add the garlic and cook for an additional minute.
Add remaining ingredients, except beans and corn. Lock lid in place, select High Pressure, 8 minutes cook time and press start.

When timer beeps, turn off pressure cooker, wait 10 minutes, then do a quick pressure release.

Remove chicken breasts from soup and dice or shred. Return chicken to soup and stir in black beans and corn.

If necessary, select Simmer and bring to a boil, stirring occasionally until beans and corn are heated.

Serve topped with shredded cheese, sour cream and tortilla strips, if desired.

# Squash Soup

Ingredients
1 onion, diced
2 garlic cloves, minced
1 carrot, diced
2 stalks celery, diced
5 lbs butternut squash, cubed
4 cups chicken broth
2 tablespoons rosemary, fresh, chopped
1 teaspoon paprika
1 teaspoon nutmeg
salt and pepper

Directions
Sweat onion and garlic in small amount of oil in pressure cooker.
Add Carrot and Celery to color before adding all remaining ingredients.
Place Pressure cooker lid on and bring to pressure over medium heat. Once rocker begins to move at medium, to cook for twenty minutes. Remove from heat, allow to depressurize on countertop.
Using hand held blender, blend to smooth consistency, adding additional broth to thin, if needed.
Add additional salt and pepper, as needed.

# Tomato Chicken Rice Soup

Ingredients
1 tablespoon olive oil
24 ounces boneless skinless chicken breasts
1 yellow onion, finely chopped
3 carrots, peeled and sliced 1/4 inch thick
3 garlic cloves, minced
1 teaspoon dried thyme
1 cup long grain rice
4 cups chicken stock
1 (28 ounce) can diced tomatoes
1 １/₂ teaspoons salt
1 teaspoon black pepper
1/4 cup fresh parsley, chopped
2 celery ribs, sliced 1/4 inch thick

Directions

Pre-heat pressure cooker on the Brown setting. Dice chicken into bite-size pieces.
Add the olive oil to the pressure cooker and brown the chicken pieces briefly, seasoning with salt and pepper.
Add the onion, carrots, celery, garlic and thyme; saute for 2 to 3 minutes.
Stir in the rice, and pour in the stock and tomatoes. Season with salt and pepper to taste.
Lock lid in place, and cook on HIGH for 8 minutes.

Reduce the pressure with the quick-release method, and carefully remove the lid. Add the parsley, adjust seasoning if needed and serve.

# Ham and Bean Stew

Ingredients
1 lb dried great northern beans
8 cups water
1 lb ham
2 teaspoons onion powder
½ teaspoon garlic powder
2 dried bay leaves
1 pinch crushed red pepper flakes
1 (10 ounce) package frozen chopped spinach
1 dash nutmeg
Fresh ground black pepper, to taste

Directions

Add washed, sorted dry beans to pressure cooker with the water.
Cut ham into small chunks and add all seasonings. Set to HIGH pressure for 20 - 25 minutes.
Use quick release method to release steam. Stir in spinach and nutmeg. Heat through and serve.

# Mediterranean Turkey Soup

Ingredients
2 teaspoons olive oil

4 Italian turkey sausage links, casings removed
1 medium onion, diced
3 cloves garlic, minced
1/2 cup pearl barley
1 cup green lentils
1 bone-in chicken breast half, skin removed
1/2 cup chopped fresh parsley
3 cups chicken stock
1 (15 ounce) can chickpeas (garbanzo beans), drained
1 (16 ounce) bag fresh spinach leaves, chopped
1 cup mild salsa

Directions

Heat 1 teaspoon olive oil in a pressure cooker over medium heat. Add sausage meat, and cook until browned, breaking it into crumbles. Remove sausage to a plate and drain oil.

Add another 1 teaspoon of olive oil to pressure cooker; cook onion and garlic until onion is transparent.

Add barley and stir 1 minute. Return sausage to pressure cooker. Add lentils, chicken, parsley, and chicken stock to cooker, adding enough stock to completely cover chicken.

Close cover securely; place pressure regulator on vent pipe. Bring pressure cooker to full pressure over high heat.

Reduce heat to medium high; cook for 9 minutes. Pressure regulator should maintain a slow steady rocking motion; adjust heat if necessary.

Remove pressure cooker from heat; use quick-release following manufacturer's instructions or allow pressure to drop on its own.

Open cooker and remove chicken; shred meat and return to soup. Add garbanzo beans, spinach and salsa; stir to blend and heat through before serving.

# Chapter 2: Pressure Cooker Main Dish Recipes

## Creamy Pressure Cooker Mushroom Chicken

Ingredients
4-6 boneless, skinless chicken breast halves
16 oz fresh white button mushrooms, thinly sliced
1/4 cup evaporated milk
1/2 cup grated Parmesan cheese
2 tablespoon cornstarch
3 tablespoon cold water
2 tablespoon fresh parsley
1 teaspoon onion powder
1 teaspoon garlic powder
Salt and pepper to taste
2 tablespoon olive oil, divided
1 medium onion, minced
6 garlic cloves, minced
2 cups low sodium chicken broth
2 tablespoon white balsamic vinegar
1 tablespoon tomato paste

1 teaspoon dried thyme
Hot cooked rice

Directions

Season the chicken breasts on both sides with onion powder, garlic powder, salt and pepper to taste. Heat 1 tablespoon olive oil over medium heat in the pressure cooker.

Add the chicken in batches and brown lightly on both sides. Remove browned chicken from the pressure cooker; place on a plate. Heat the remaining 1 tablespoon olive oil in the pressure cooker over medium heat.

Add the onions and sauté for 2 minutes or until translucent. Add the garlic; cook and stir for 30 seconds. Stir in the chicken broth, vinegar, tomato paste and thyme. Place the rack in the pressure cooker; put the browned chicken on the rack. Add the sliced mushrooms.

Put the cover on the pressure and lock in place. Place the regulator on top if the pressure cooker uses one. When the pressure cooker reaches high pressure - 15 psi, set a timer and cook for 6 minutes.

Using the Quick Pressure Release method recommended for your pressure cooker, release pressure and remove the cover. Remove chicken and keep warm. Stir the evaporated milk, and Parmesan cheese into the sauce.

Combine the cornstarch and water, whisking until smooth. Stir the cornstarch mixture into the sauce and cook over medium/low heat, stirring constantly, until the sauce thickens. Stir in the chopped parsley.
Pour the sauce over the chicken and serve over rice.

# Easy Pressure Cooker Butter Chicken

Ingredients
10 boneless skinless chicken thighs
2 tablespoons fresh ginger root, peeled and chopped
1/2 cup (1 stick) unsalted butter
2 teaspoons ground cumin
1 tablespoon paprika
2 teaspoons kosher salt
3/4 cup heavy cream
2 (14-oz) cans diced tomatoes and juice
2 jalapeno peppers, seeded and chopped
3/4 cup Greek yogurt
2 teaspoons garam masala
2 teaspoons ground roasted cumin seeds
2 tablespoons cornstarch
2 tablespoons water
1/4 cup firmly packed minced cilantro

Directions
Cut the chicken pieces into quarters.
Put tomatoes, jalapeno and ginger in a blender or food processor and blend to a fine puree.
Add butter to pressure cooking pot, select Browning. When butter is melted and foam begins to subside, add the chicken pieces, a few at a time, and sear until they are nicely browned all over for about 2-3 minutes per

batch. Remove them with a slotted spoon into a bowl and put aside.

Add ground cumin and paprika to the butter in the pot and cook, stirring rapidly, for 10-15 seconds. Add the tomato mixture, salt, cream, yogurt and chicken pieces along with any juices that have accumulated in the bowl to the pot.

Gently stir the chicken to coat the pieces. Cover and lock lid in place. Select High Pressure and 5 minutes cook time. When timer beeps, turn off and use a natural pressure release for 10 minutes. After 10 minutes use a quick pressure release to release any remaining pressure.

Stir in the garam masala and roasted cumin. Whisk together cornstarch and water in a small bowl. Stir in to sauce in the pot. Select sauté and bring to a boil. Turn off pressure cooker and stir in minced cilantro.

Serve with rice.

# Beef Short Ribs

Ingredients
4 large beef short ribs
2 tablespoons vegetable oil
2 slices bacon, finely chopped
1 large onion finely chopped
3 garlic cloves, minced or pressed
1/2 cup apple juice or dry red wine
1 cup beef both
2 tablespoons tomato paste
1 tablespoon cornstarch
1 tablespoon water

Directions
Season ribs generously with salt and pepper. Add oil to the pressure cooking pot, select Browning. When oil is hot, brown the ribs in small batches, do not overfill. Remove to a plate.
Add bacon to pressure cooking pot and cook until brown and crisp. Add onion to pressure cooking pot and sauté until tender for about 3 minutes. Add garlic and cook one minute more.
Add the apple juice and use a wooden spoon to scrape up any brown bits stuck on the bottom of the pot. Add beef broth, tomato paste, and ribs to pressure cooking pot, cover and lock lid in place. Select High Pressure and 40 minutes cook time. When timer beeps do a

natural pressure release for 10 minutes and then release any remaining pressure.

With tongs, remove ribs to a plate or bowl and cover with foil to keep warm. Use a fat separator and a mesh strainer to separate the fat from the juices. Return juices to the cooking pot.

In a small bowl, combine cornstarch and water. Add to juices in the cooking pot. Select Sauté and bring to a boil, stirring constantly until juices thicken. Turn pressure cooker off.

Add ribs and stir to coat with the sauce. Put the lid back on the pressure cooker and allow the ribs to absorb some of the sauce for about 10 minutes stirring occasionally if sauce is still bubbling and serve.

# Honey Mustard Pork Chops

Ingredients
4 medium cut Bone-in Pork Chops
½ cup onions, thinly sliced
3 tablespoons minced garlic
8 oz white button mushrooms, sliced
4 cups fresh green beans, chopped
2 cups chicken broth
3 Tablespoons cornstarch
¼ cup honey
½ cup dijon mustard
½ teaspoon salt
¼ teaspoon black pepper
1 tablespoon olive oil

Directions
Turn pressure cooker to sauté. Add olive oil and when pot is hot sear both sides of each pork chop. Remove seared pork chops from pot.

Pressure cooker still on sauté add, onions, and garlic, cook for 1-2 minutes. In a small bowl reserve ¼ cup of chicken broth and whisk in 2 Tablespoons cornstarch. Pour remaining 1¾ cups of chicken broth into pressure cooker, slowly whisk in cornstarch mixture.

Stir in honey and mustard, salt and pepper. Add in the seared pork chops, mushrooms, and green beans in that order.

Lock lid and close pressure valve. Cook on High Pressure for 8-10 minutes.

Allow a 10-12 minute natural release. Remove green beans, mushrooms and pork chops from pressure cooker.

Turn Pressure Cooker back to sauté, whisk in remaining tablespoon of cornstarch to thicken sauce even more.

# Chunky Beef Stew

Ingredients
1 1/2 lbs. beef stew meat
3 tbsp oil
1 can green beans with liquid
2 cans diced tomatoes with liquid
2 tbsp cornstarch
1/3 cup cold water
2 large potatoes
4-5 large carrots
1 large onion
Salt and pepper to taste

Directions
Cut the beef stew meat into bite size pieces. Do the same with the potatoes, carrots and onions.
Heat the pressure cooker over medium high heat. Add the oil and stew meat. Stir and cook until the meat is well browned all over. Add the potatoes, carrots, onion, beans with their liquid, and tomatoes with their liquid. Add salt and pepper to taste.
Place the lid and weight on the pressure cooker according to your manufacturer's instruction. Heat on medium high setting until pressure is achieved. Continue cooking for 15 minutes.
At the end of the 15 minutes cooking time, reduce the pressure immediately by running cold water on the top

of the pressure cooker. When pressure releases, open the top of the cooker and place it back on the stove. Combine the cornstarch and cold water in a small bowl. Bring the stew back up to the boil, add the cornstarch and water and stir until thickened and serve.

# Teriyaki Chicken

Ingredients
1/4 cup low sodium soy sauce
3 tbsp rice wine
2 tbsp honey
2 cloves garlic
1 teaspoon fresh grated ginger
1 teaspoon siracha hot sauce
8 drumsticks (28 oz), skin removed
1 tbsp sesame seeds
Chopped scallions

Directions
Use saute button, when hot add soy sauce, rice wine, honey, garlic, ginger and sriracha and cook 2 minutes, stirring.
Add the chicken, cover and lock the lid. Cook on high pressure 15 to 20 minutes until the chicken is tender.
When pressure releases, finish with scallions and sesame seeds.

# Juicy Pressure Cooker Pot Roast

Ingredients
3 1/2 lb beef chuck roast
1 tablespoon vegetable oil
1 large onion, roughly chopped
1 1/2 cup water or beef broth
2 bay leaves

Directions
Pat roast dry and season liberally with lemon pepper and seasonings of your choice.
Put oil in the cooking pot and select browning. When oil begins to sizzle, brown meat on both sides. Remove roast from the cooking pot and add onions, water and bay leaves. Put roast back in the cooking pot on top of the onions.
Select High Pressure. Set timer for 70 minutes. When timer sounds turn off pressure cooker and use a natural pressure release to release pressure for approximately 20 minutes. When valve drops carefully remove the lid.
Remove roast to a serving dish. Strain juices and discard onion and bay leaves. Thicken juices in cooking pot on simmer with some water and flour or cornstarch to make gravy.

# Lemon Salmon

Ingredients
4 salmon fillets
2 tablespoons olive oil
1 teaspoon garlic, minced
2 anchovy fillets (optional) or 2 teaspoons anchove paste
1/2 teaspoon crushed red pepper
1 tablespoon butter
1 cup loosely pack parsley
juice and zest of 1 lemon
2 tablespoons capers
1 tablespoon olive oil
1 shallot, finely minced
1 cup long-grain rice
1 1/4 cups broth
1/4 cup lemon juice
1/2 cup white wine
1 teaspoon sea salt
1 tablespoon parsley, chopped
zest of 1 lemon
sea salt and ground pepper
lemon slices
Directions
Combine olive oil, garlic, anchovy (if using), crushed red pepper, and butter in a small saute pan over medium-

high heat. Saute until the mixture is fragrant and garlic is golden, set aside.

To the bowl of a small food processor, add the parsley, juice and zest of 1 lemon, and capers. Spoon the olive oil and garlic mixture over top. Pulse until finely chopped. Scoop into a small bowl until ready to serve.

Add the olive oil and shallot to the pressure cooker. Saute until fragrant. Add rice. Cook 1-2 minutes. Add liquid, parsley, zest, salt and pepper.

Salt and pepper salmon portions on both sides. Place on steamer basket, and top with lemon slices. Set in the pressure cooker over the rice and liquid.

Lock pressure cooker. Set on rice setting, or about 4 minutes if using a stove top model. Remove from heat source if using a stove top model. Wait 5 minutes, then de-pressurize.

Lift steamer basket from pressure cooker. Fluff rice with a fork.

To serve, drizzle the Lemon Caper Chimichurri over the salmon and rice.

# Garlic Honey Chicken

Ingredients
3 pounds boneless, skinless chicken thighs
1/2 teaspoon dried minced garlic
1 teaspoons Sriracha chili garlic sauce
3/4 cup soy sauce
3/4 cup ketchup
3/4 cup honey
2 tablespoons cornstarch
2 tablespoons water
1 tablespoon chopped fresh basil

Directions
Add garlic, chili sauce, soy sauce, ketchup and honey to pressure cooking pot. Stir to combine. Add chicken to the pot. Cover pot and lock lid in place.
Select High Pressure and 9 minutes cook time.
After cooking for 9 minutes, turn off pressure cooker and use a quick pressure release.

In a small bowl, dissolve cornstarch in 2 tablespoons water. Add cornstarch mixture to the sauce in the pot stirring constantly. Select Simmer and bring to a boil, stirring constantly. After sauce thickens, add fresh basil to the sauce.

# Lime Chicken Thighs

Ingredients
Juice and zest of 1 lime
3 garlic cloves, minced
1 teaspoon cumin
1 teaspoon chili powder
2 tablespoons olive oil divided
1/4 cup fresh cilantro, chopped
4 chicken thighs, about 1-1/2 pounds (I used bone in, skin on)
1/2 cup chicken stock
1 tablespoon arrowroot powder, tapioca starch or corn starch
Salt and pepper to taste

Directions
Place 1 tablespoon olive oil, lime juice, garlic, cumin, chili powder, cilantro and salt and pepper in a plastic ziploc or large glass dish and mix. Pat the chicken dry and add to the marinade. Allow to sit for at least 30 minutes, or up to 2 hours.

Set your pressure cooker to sauté and once hot, add the other tablespoon of olive oil. Remove the chicken from the marinade and add to the pot. Let it sear a few minutes on each side until it's golden. Then add 1/2 cup chicken stock, close the pot with the lid, and push the poultry button, and cook for 12 minutes..

Add the arrowroot powder to 2 tablespoons of cold water. Once the chicken is done, remove it from the pot, and hit sauté again. Add the arrowroot mixture.

Whisk the ingredients in the pan, making sure to pick up any fond from the chicken. Season as necessary. Once the sauce is thick and combined, turn the pot off. Serve the chili lime chicken with sauce immediately.

## Pressure Cooker Tips:

1. The less amount of liquid is needed than traditional cooking methods.
2. Extreme caution must used when pressure cooker contain hot liquids. Do not touch hot surfaces. Use handles.
3. Never exceed the Maximum Fill Amount of the pressure cooker.
4. Do not open pressure cooker until cool.
5. Do not open pressure cooker until inside pressure has been released. Do not force it open.
6. Do not use pressure cooker for frying with oil.
7. Do not place the pressure cooker in heated oven.
8. Always check air vent to be sure it moves freely before the use.

# 1-Lemon Marinated Tuna

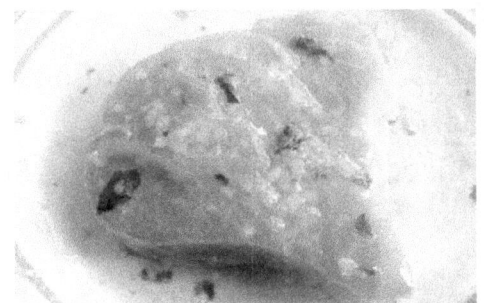

Total Time: 35 minutes

Serves: 4 Servings

Ingredients:

- 1 pound tuna steak, 1-inch thick
- 1 tbsp soy sauce
- ¼ cup lemon juice
- 2 tbsp olive oil
- 2 cloves garlic, minced
- 1 tsp ginger
- ½ tsp black pepper
- ½ cup water

Cooking Directions:

1. Place tuna steaks in a shallow glass dish.
2. Combine remaining ingredients except water.
3. Add mixture over tuna and marinate for 30 minutes, turning tuna once.
4. Remove tuna from marinade mixture and place on rack in cooker.
5. Pour marinade and water into cooker. Place pressure cooker over medium-high heat and cook 3 minutes. Cool cooker at once.
6. Serve over steam rice and enjoy.

Nutritional Value (Amount per Serving): **Calories 170 g, Cholesterol 52mg, Fat 6g.**

# 2-Pressure Cooker Carrot Soup with Cream

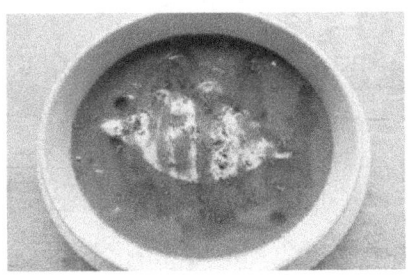

Total Time: 40 minutes

Serves: 14 Servings

Ingredients

- 1/4 cup butter
- 6 cloves garlic
- 5 cups baby carrots
- 8 cups vegetable stock
- 3 cups heavy whipping cream
- 1/2 tsp curry powder
- 2 cups onions, diced
- 1 cups chopped celery
- 5 green onions, chopped
- 1 potato, diced
- Black pepper
- Salt

Cooking Directions

1. Melt the butter in the pressure cooker over medium heat.
2. Sauté the onion in hot butter until onions become translucent, about 10 minutes.
3. Now add green onions, celery, potato, and garlic. Cook until it tender, 5 minutes.
4. Add vegetable stock and carrot then increase heat to high.
5. Place lid on pressure cooker and lock.
6. Reduce the heat to medium-high and cook for 6 minutes.
7. Wait the cooker to release pressure and remove the lid. Return cooker to stove.
8. Mix curry powder and cream into soup.
9. Puree soup with a blender until completely smooth.
10. Season with pepper and salt. Serve hot and enjoy.

**Nutritional Value (Amount per Serving):** Calories **290** kcal, Total Fat **25.8** g, Cholesterol **89** mg, Carbohydrate **15** g, Protein **3.6** g, Sodium **380** mg.

# 3-Chicken Curry with Tomato

Total Time: 60 minutes

Serves: 6 Servings

Ingredients

- 1 cup yogurt
- 1 onion, chopped into wedges
- 2 tomatoes, chopped
- 8 tbsp spicy curry paste
- 2 kg boneless chicken thighs, cut each into 3 pieces
- 1 tbsp oil
- Chopped coriander, for garnish

Cooking Directions

1. Mix the spicy curry paste and yogurt in a bowl.

2. Then add chicken thighs and coat evenly and cover bowl with lid and place into the refrigerator for 25 minutes to marinate.
3. Heat 1 tbsp oil in the cooker.
4. Add onion wedges in cooker and sauté until golden, for about 10 minutes.
5. Add marinated chicken thigh and chopped tomatoes in pressure cooker and sealed the pressure cooker with lid and cook for 20 minutes on high pressure.
6. Garnish chicken curry with chopped corianders and serve over steam rice and enjoy.

**Nutritional Value (Amount per Serving):** Calories **420** kcal, Total Fat **15.3** g, Cholesterol **230** mg, Carbohydrate **14.2** g, Protein **53** g, Sodium **260** mg.

# 4-Quick Pressure Cooker Brown Rice

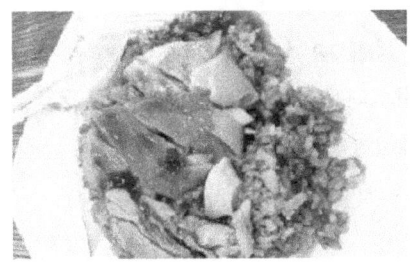

Total Time: 20 minutes

Serves: 2 Servings

Ingredients

- 1 cup brown rice
- 2 cups water
- 1 tbsp mix seasoning
- 2 chicken bouillon cubes
- 1 1/2 tbsp butter
- Pepper

Cooking Directions

1. Spray cooker with cooking oil and add all ingredients in pressure cooker.
2. Once pressure is acquired, and then set timer for 15 minutes.

3. Let the pressure cooker cool completely and didn't open lid until ready to serve.
4. This will maintain nice consistency of rice.

**Nutritional Value (Amount per Serving):** Calories **85** kcal, Total Fat **9.1** g, Cholesterol **23** mg, Carbohydrate **1.2** g, Protein **2** g, Sodium **680** mg.

# 5-Pressure Cooker Pasta with Cheese

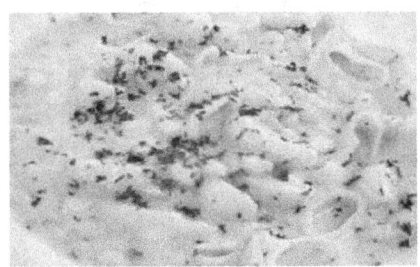

Total Time: 26 minutes

Serves: 4 Servings
Ingredients

- 1 1/2 cups water
- 2 tbsp butter
- 1 1/2 cups chicken broth
- 230g pasta
- 1 tbsp parmesan cheese, grated
- 1 tsp mustard
- ½ cup sweet corn
- 6 fluid oz whipping cream
- 2 cup shredded Cheddar cheese
- 6 oz cream cheese
- Chopped parsley, garnish
- Pepper
- salt

Cooking Directions

1. Add water, chicken broth, pasta, Cheddar cheese, sweet corn, cream cheese, butter, Parmesan cheese, mustard, black pepper and salt in a pressure cooker.
2. Seal pressure cooker with a lid and bring to high heat.
3. Once the full pressure is reached, cook for 6 minutes.
4. Release pressure quick-release method.
5. Garnish pasta with chopped parsley and serve hot.

**Nutritional Value (Amount per Serving):** Calories **445** kcal, Total Fat **40** g, Cholesterol **120** mg, Carbohydrate **3** g, Protein **18** g, Sodium **840** mg.

# 6-Portabella Risotto

Total Time: 30 minutes

Serves: 2 Servings
Ingredients

- 2 cups chicken broth
- 1 cup parmesan cheese, grated
- 1 garlic cloves, minced
- 4 oz portabella mushrooms, sliced
- 1 cup risotto rice
- 2 tbsp olive oil
- 2 tbsp butter
- 1/2 onion, diced

Cooking Directions

1. Add 2 tbsp oil and 1 tbsp Butter in pressure cooker and turn on heat.

2. Add garlic and onion in cooker and sauté until translucent.
3. Add rice and mushrooms in cooker. Mix until rice is coated well with oil.
4. Then add Chicken broth.
5. Cover the cooker with lid and cook on high pressure for 6 minutes.
6. Release pressure and add remaining 1 tbsp butter in cooker.
7. Mix parmesan cheese and serve.

**Nutritional Value (Amount per Serving):** Calories **626** kcal, Total Fat **27** g, Cholesterol **31** mg, Carbohydrate **80** g, Protein **13** g, Sodium **854** mg.

# 7-Simple Lentil Soup

Total Time: 35 minutes
Serves: 2 Servings
Ingredients

- 1/2 tsp ground cumin
- 2 cups vegetable broth
- 1 tablespoons olive oil
- 1/2 cup dry lentils, rinsed and picked
- 1 carrots, chopped
- 1 celery ribs, chopped
- 1 small onion, chopped
- 2 garlic cloves, minced
- 2 bay leaves
- Pepper
- Salt

Cooking Directions

1. In your pressure cooker, sauté the garlic and chopped onion in the oil until onions are translucent.
2. Add celery and carrots and sauté for 2 minutes. Then add the ground cumin and mix well.
3. Add vegetable broth, bay leaves and lentils, sealed the pressure cooker with lid, and bring up to pressure.
4. Cook for 22 minutes.
5. Open the pressure cooker using quick release method.
6. Take out the bay leaves.
7. Season with pepper and salt to taste.
8. Serve hot and enjoy.

**Nutritional Value (Amount per Serving):** Calories **301** kcal, Total Fat **9.1** g, Carbohydrate **37** g, Protein **18.2** g, Sodium **867** mg.

# 8-Pressure Cooker Spicy Chickpeas Curry

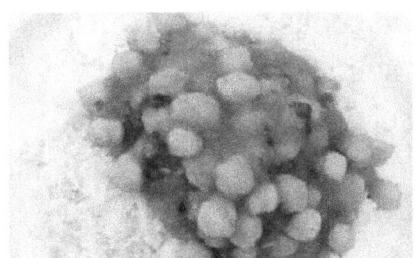

Total Time: 30 minutes

Serves: 4 Servings
Ingredients

- 1 tbsp vegetable oil
- 1 tsp ground cumin
- 1/2 tsp garam masala
- 1/2 tsp ground turmeric
- 1 tsp cumin seeds
- 1 onion, chopped
- 1 garlic clove, minced
- 1/2 tsp chili powder
- 1 tsp ground coriander
- 1 cup water
- sprig of coriander, to garnish
- 200g tin chickpeas, rinsed and drained
- 200g tin tomatoes
- 1 potato, diced
- Salt

Cooking Directions

1. In a pressure cooker, heat oil on medium heat.
2. Add cumin seeds in cooker and stir for 40 seconds until they pop.
3. Add in chopped onion. Sauté for 3 minutes.
4. Add in minced garlic and other spices. Cook, stirring frequently for 2 minutes.
5. Add in tomatoes, chickpeas and potatoes, together with 1 cup of water.
6. Add salt to taste.
7. Seal cooker with lid and bring to pressure over high heat.
8. Once it reaches pressure reduce heat and cook for 15 minutes.
9. Release pressure through natural release method.
10. Garnish dish with chopped coriander.
11. Serve with steamed rice.

**Nutritional Value (Amount per Serving):** Calories **225** kcal, Total Fat **6**g, Carbohydrate **34** g, Protein **8.2** g.

# 9-Mashed Potatoes

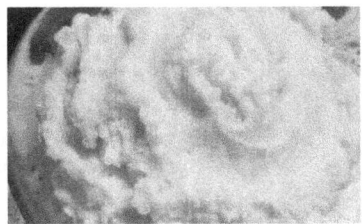

Total Time: 57 minutes
Serves: 4 Servings
Ingredients

- 1400g russet potatoes, sliced
- 1/4 cup butter
- 2 cup water
- 1/2 tsp black pepper
- 1/2 cup milk
- 2 tsp salt

Cooking Directions

1. Pour water in pressure cooker to a boil over high heat.
2. When water is boiling, add potatoes and seal lid and bring cooker over high pressure.
3. Reduce heat and cook for 32 minutes.
4. Release pressure quick-release method. Drain potatoes and return them into pressure cooker.

5. Add milk and butter and cover cooker with lid for 6 minutes.
6. Allow the heat from the potatoes to warm the milk and melt the butter.
7. Open lid and season with white pepper and salt.
8. Use hand masher to mash potatoes until lumps are remove.
9. Transfer into bowl and serve hot.

**Nutritional Value (Amount per Serving):** Calories **360** kcal, Total Fat **12** g, Carbohydrate **56** g, Protein **7** g, Sodium 1204 mg.

# 10-Pressure Cooker Tomato Basil Soup

Total Time: 25 minutes
Serves: 4 Servings
Ingredients

- 1 tsp red chili flakes
- 1 cup grated parmesan cheese
- 14 oz canned tomato puree
- 7 oz caned diced tomatoes, un-drained
- 1 1/2 tbsp olive oil
- 1 onion, chopped
- 1 garlic clove, minced
- 1 small carrot, chopped
- 3 cups chicken broth
- 4 oz cheese tortellini
- 1/2 cup fresh basil, minced
- Black pepper, ground
- Salt

Cooking Directions

1. In a pressure cooker, heat the oil over medium-high heat.
2. Add onion and sauté until softened about 4 minutes.
3. Add minced garlic and cook, 60 seconds.
4. Add chopped carrot, chicken broth and chili flakes. Mix in the tomato puree, diced tomatoes with juice and tortellini.
5. Sealed with lid. And bring cooker over high heat.
6. When it reaches high pressure, then reduce heat and cook for 6 minutes.
7. Release the pressure with natural Release method.
8. Mix in the basil and let stand for 3 minutes.
9. Season with pepper and salt to taste.
10. Sprinkle grated parmesan cheese and serve hot.

**Nutritional Value (Amount per Serving):** Calories **180** kcal, Total Fat **8** g, Carbohydrate **19** g, Protein **8** g, Sodium **709** mg.

# 11-Pressure Cooker Lemon Chicken with Cheese

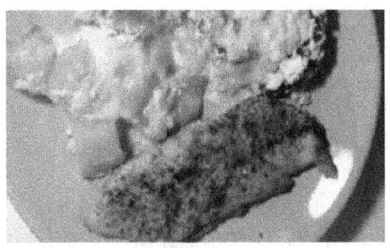

Total Time: 20 minutes
Serves: 3 Servings
Ingredients

- 1 tbsp olive oil
- 3 boneless and skinless chicken breast
- 1/2 tsp ground cumin
- 1 cup spicy salsa
- 1/2 tsp red chili powder
- ¼ cup fresh lime juice
- 4 oz goat cheese, crumbled

Cooking Directions

1. In a pressure cooker, heat the oil over medium-high heat until hot.
2. Place the chicken breast in cooker for lightly brown both the sides.

3. Transfer chicken to a plate.
4. Add cumin, salsa, chili powder and lime juice to the cooker. Stir well and return the chicken into the cooker.
5. Sealed cooker with lid and bring over the high heat.
6. When it reaches high pressure, reduce the heat and cook for 6 minutes.
7. Open the pressure cooker using quick release method.
8. Transfer chicken breast and its sauce to a plate of steam rice and sprinkle crumbled cheese and serve.

**Nutritional Value (Amount per Serving):** Calories **214** kcal, Total Fat **18** g, Carbohydrate **2** g, Protein **11** g, Sodium **136** mg.

# 12-Pressure cooker Strawberry Jam

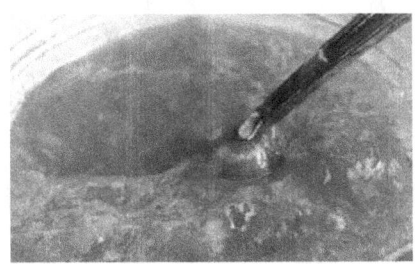

Total Time: 70 minutes
Serves: 2 Servings
Ingredients

- 2 cups strawberries
- 1 1/2 cup granulated sugar
- 1/4 cup lemon juice

Cooking Directions

1. Rinse the strawberries and cut into half.
2. Add sugar and strawberries in pressure cooker and set aside for 60 minutes.
3. Use masher and mash the strawberries until dissolved in sugar then add lemon juice and mix well.
4. Sealed the pressure cooker with the lid and bring over high heat for 6 minutes.

5. Remove from heat and release pressure using natural pressure release method.
6. Remove the lid and return to high heat for 3 minutes until jam reaches gel consistency.
7. Allow jam to completely cool then pour into jar and refrigerate for a week.

**Nutritional Value (Amount per Serving):** Calories **616** kcal, Total Fat **1** g, Carbohydrate **161** g, Protein **1** g, Sodium **8** mg.

# 13-Pressure Cooker Split Peas

Total Time: 20 minutes
Serves: 2 Servings
Ingredients

- 1 tbsp olive oil
- 1 red chili pepper, diced
- 1 garlic clove, minced
- 1/2 tsp garam masala
- 1/4 tsp ground turmeric
- 1/2 tsp dry mustard
- 1 cup dried yellow split peas
- 1 tomato, chopped
- Pinch of asafetida
- 1/4 cup plain yogurt
- 1 tsp butter
- 1 onion, chopped
- 2 tsp ginger, grated
- 2 cups water
- Chopped corianders

Cooking Directions

1. Rinse yellow split peas.
2. Heat oil in pressure cooker and add asafetida and dry mustard. Stir 60 seconds.
3. Add onions and garlic and sauté until onion soften.
4. Add all other ingredients expect from corianders, garam masala and salt to pressure cooker.
5. Sealed the cooker with Lid and bring up to pressure.
6. Reduce the heat and cook for 10 minutes.
7. Release pressure using quick release pressure method.
8. Add garam- masala and salt stir well. Garnish with chopped corianders.
9. Serve with pita or hot rice.

**Nutritional Value (Amount per Serving):** Calories **476** kcal, Total Fat **10** g, Carbohydrate **70** g, Protein **27** g, Sodium **1220** mg.

# 14-Pressure Cooker Rice with Peas

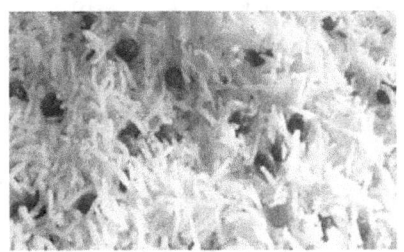

Total Time: 25 minutes
Serves: 2 Servings
Ingredients

- 1/2 cup rice
- 1/2 cup frozen peas
- 2 cups chicken stock
- 2 tbsp butter
- 1 onion, chopped
- 1/4 cup parmesan cheese
- Pepper

Cooking Directions

1. In cooker, heat 1 1/2 tbsp butter over medium heat.
2. Sauté onions for 5 minutes until soften. Stir frequently.
3. Add rice, and sauté until slightly brown.
4. Add frozen peas and chicken stock and stir well.

5. Sealed cooker with lid and bring to pressure. Lower heat and cook for 14 minutes.
6. Release pressure and open the lid.
7. Add remaining half tbsp of butter, pepper and parmesan cheese.
8. Wait for minute until cheese and butter melts.
9. Mix well and serve hot.

**Nutritional Value (Amount per Serving):** Calories **334** kcal, Total Fat **12** g, Carbohydrate **48** g, Protein **6** g, Sodium **870** mg.

# 15-Pressure Cooker BBQ Sauce

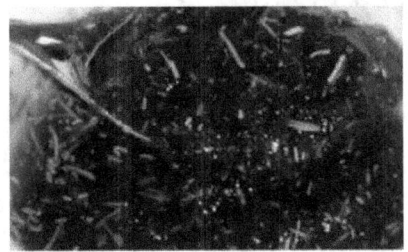

Total Time: 25 minutes
Serves: 3 Servings
Ingredients

- 2 cup ketchup
- 1/4 cup Worcestershire sauce
- 1/8 cup molasses
- 1/8 cup mustard, prepare
- 1/4 cup vinegar
- 1 tbsp BBQ seasoning
- 1/4 cup light brown sugar
- 1/2 tsp ground black pepper
- Salt

Cooking Directions

1. Add all ingredients in pressure cooker. Mix well.
2. Sealed with lid and bring to low pressure for 20 minutes.
3. Release pressure using quick release method.

4. Add extra seasoning for taste and mix well.
5. Pour into jar and cover with airtight lid and refrigerate for month.

**Nutritional Value (Amount per Serving):** Calories **226** kcal, Total Fat 0.5 g, Carbohydrate **56** g, Protein **2**g, Sodium **2012** mg.

# 16-Quick Beef Stew

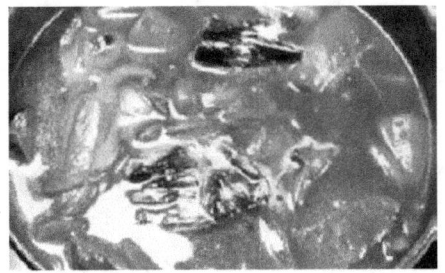

Total Time: 35 minutes
Serves: 4 Servings
Ingredients

- 1 tbsp oil
- 1 onion, diced
- 1 cube beef bouillon
- 1 cup water
- 1 tsp cornstarch
- 450g cubed beef stew meat
- 2 carrots, diced
- 4 medium potatoes, cubed
- 1 tsp salt

Cooking Directions

1. In a pressure cooker heat the oil over medium-high heat.
2. Add diced onion and beef, and sauté until browned.

3. Add the water, carrots and beef cubes, sealed with the lid, and bring to medium heat for 20 minutes.
4. In pan place the potatoes with enough water and bring to a boil, for 10 minutes or until tender. Drain.
5. Release the pressure using quick release method.
6. Open a lid, and place cooker over medium heat bring to a boil.
7. Add cornstarch into little amount of cold water and mix into the stew and cook for few minutes.
8. Add boil potatoes in the stew and mix well.
9. Serve hot and enjoy.

**Nutritional Value (Amount per Serving):** Calories **205** kcal, Total Fat **3** g, Carbohydrate **39** g, Protein **4g**, Sodium **771** mg.

# 17-Pressure Cooker BBQ Chicken

Total Time: 25 minutes
Serves: 4 Servings
Ingredients

- 2 tbsp olive oil
- 2 tbsp BBQ sauce
- 1 onion, chopped
- 1/4 cup chili sauce
- 450g boneless, skinless chicken thighs
- 1/2 tsp ground paprika
- 1/4 cup water
- 1 tbsp vinegar
- Coriander, chopped
- Ground black pepper
- Salt

Cooking Directions

1. In a pressure cooker heat the oil over medium heat. Add chicken and cook until browned for 3 minutes per side.
2. Sprinkle ground black pepper, paprika and salt onto chicken.
3. Combine chopped onion, chili sauce, BBQ sauce, water and vinegar in bowl and pour over chicken.
4. Close pressure cooker with lid and cook for 15 minutes.
5. Release pressure through natural release method.
6. Open lid and sprinkle chopped coriander over chicken and serve hot.

**Nutritional Value (Amount per Serving):** Calories **300** kcal, Total Fat **15** g, Carbohydrate **5** g, Protein **33**g, Sodium **605** mg.

# 18-Pressure Cooker Apple Sauce

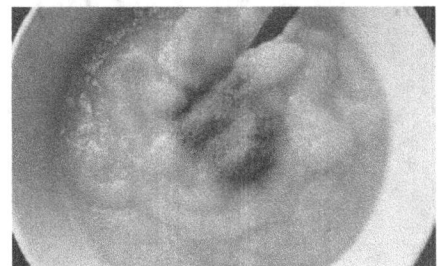

Total Time: 25 minutes
Serves: 4 Servings
Ingredients

- 8 apples, cored and cut into small pieces
- 1 tsp ground cinnamon
- 2/4 cup water
- 1 cup dried cranberries
- 1 lemon juice

Cooking Directions

1. In a pressure cooker, combine all the ingredients.
2. Close cooker with a lid and bring to high heat.
3. When it reaches high pressure, reduce the heat and cook for 3 minutes.
4. Release pressure through natural release method. Let cool for 15 minutes.
5. Use blender and blend until get soft puree or you desired consistency.

6. Let cool completely and store in airtight container in the refrigerator up to 4 days.

**Nutritional Value (Amount per Serving):** Calories **206** kcal, Total Fat **1** g, Carbohydrate **53** g, Protein **1**g, Sodium **4** mg.

# 19-Pressure Cooker Mix Fruit Risotto

Total Time: 25 minutes
Serves: 6 Servings
Ingredients

- 2 tbsp butter, unsalted
- 1/4 cup sugar
- Grated 1 lemon zest
- 2 tsp vanilla extract
- 1 cup medium grain rice
- 1 can coconut milk, unsweetened
- 1 cup whole milk
- 2 cups fresh strawberries, blackberries, sliced mango, pineapple chunks

Cooking Directions

1. In a pressure cooker, melt the butter over medium heat.

2. Add the rice and cook for 1 minute, stirring constantly.
3. Add the milk, coconut milk, sugar and vanilla and lemon zest mix well and bring to a boil.
4. Sealed with lid and place high heat when cooker reaches high pressure, reduce heat and cook for 7 minutes.
5. Remove the cooker from heat and release the pressure through natural release method. Let cool for 15 minutes.
6. Let the risotto completely cool then add mix fruits and mix well.
7. Serve chill and enjoy.

**Nutritional Value (Amount per Serving):** Calories **221** kcal, Total Fat **5** g, Carbohydrate **38** g, Protein **3**g, Sodium **46** mg.

# 20-Rice Pudding with Blueberries

Total Time: 30 minutes
Serves: 4 Servings
Ingredients

- 1 cup almond milk
- 1/2 cup medium grain rice
- 1 cup blueberries
- 1 tsp vanilla extract
- 1 cup coconut milk
- 1 cup water
- 3 tbsp sugar
- Pinch of salt

Cooking Directions

1. In a pressure cooker, Add rice, almond milk, water, sugar, coconut milk and salt.
2. Seal with the lid and place over the high heat. When it reaches high pressure reduce the heat and cook for 10 minutes.

3. Remove the cooker from heat and release the pressure through natural release method. Let cool for 15 minutes.
4. Add blueberries and vanilla extract and simmer the pudding, over low heat for 5 minutes.
5. Transfer the pudding in bowl Cover with lid and place into the refrigerator for chill before serving.

**Nutritional Value (Amount per Serving):** Calories **418** kcal, Total Fat **28** g, Carbohydrate **39** g, Protein **4**g, Sodium **60** mg.

# 21-Pressure Cooker Sweet Potatoes

Total Time: 20 minutes

Serves: 6 Servings

Ingredients

- 2/3 cup brown sugar
- 4 tbsp butter, unsalted
- 6 small sweet potatoes, ends trimmed
- 1/2 cup water
- Pinch of salt

Cooking Directions

1. Place the potatoes in pressure cooker and fill with the water.
2. Sealed with the lid and place over high heat when it reaches high pressure reduces the heat and cook for 9 minutes.
3. Remove the cooker from the heat. Release the pressure through quick release method.

4. Check the potatoes should be tender. Drain water.
5. When it cool completely, slip off the skins and cut into 3/4 inch thick slices and Set aside.
6. In a large pan, add the brown sugar, butter, salt and water.
7. Melt over medium heat, stirring constantly.
8. When it become smooth then add sliced potatoes and stir until all slices evenly coat with mixture for 3 minutes.
9. Transfer into the serving bowl and Serve.

**Nutritional Value (Amount per Serving):** Calories **129** kcal, Total Fat **7** g, Carbohydrate **15** g, Protein **1**g, Sodium **87** mg.

# 22-Pressure Cooker Roasted Potatoes

Total Time: 25 minutes
Serves: 4 Servings
Ingredients

- 20 baby potatoes, cut into 2 inches
- 5 tbsp olive oil
- 1/2 cup vegetable stock
- 1/2 tsp sweet paprika
- 1/2 tsp dried herbs
- 1 tbsp chopped green onions
- 1 tbsp parmesan cheese, grated
- Black pepper
- Salt, to taste

Cooking Directions

1. In a pressure cooker heat olive oil over medium-high heat.

2. Add potatoes in cooker and sauté until brown on all sides.
3. Add vegetable stock in pressure cooker.
4. Sealed with lid and place over the high heat. When it reaches high pressure, reduce the heat and cook for 5 minutes.
5. Remove the cooker from the heat. Release the pressure through natural release method.
6. Open the lid potatoes should be tender and soft.
7. Drain and sprinkle salt to taste.
8. Add dried herbs, sweet paprika, chopped onion, and black pepper and mix well.
9. Transfer potatoes into serving bowl and garnish with grated parmesan cheese and Serve.

**Nutritional Value (Amount per Serving):** Calories **117** kcal, Total Fat **51** g, Carbohydrate **0.5** g, Protein **0.1**g, Sodium **39** mg.

# 23-Pressure Cooker Lentils with Spinach

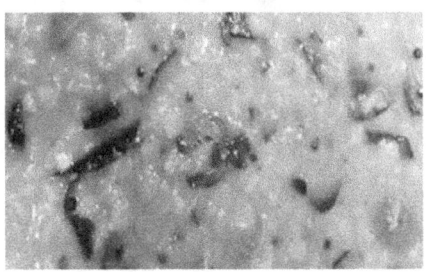

Total Time: 20 minutes
Serves: 4 Servings
Ingredients

- 2 tbsp oil
- 1 onion, chopped
- 1 tbsp ginger, grated
- 1/2 tsp ground turmeric
- 1 garlic clove, minced
- 2 fresh diced tomatoes
- 2 cups vegetable stock
- 1 cup dried brown lentils, rinsed
- 1 cup fresh chopped spinach
- Chopped fresh coriander, for serving
- Black pepper
- Salt

Cooking Directions

1. In a pressure cooker, heat the oil over medium-high heat.
2. Add onion and sauté until soften for 2 minutes.
3. Add the ginger, garlic turmeric and stir for 30 seconds.
4. Add chopped tomatoes, vegetable stock and lentils. Mix well until combine.
5. Sealed with lid and place over the high heat. When it reaches high pressure then reduce heat and for 10 minutes.
6. Remove the Cooker from heat. Release the pressure through quick release method.
7. Open the lid. Add salt and pepper to taste.
8. Add spinach and simmer, over medium heat for 3 minutes.
9. Sprinkling of chopped coriander and serve hot.

**Nutritional Value (Amount per Serving):** Calories **91** kcal, Total Fat **7** g, Carbohydrate **6** g, Protein **1.1**g, Sodium **49** mg.

# 24-Pressure Cooker Kidney Beans Stew

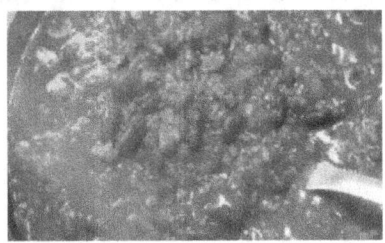

Total Time: 25 minutes
Serves: 4 Servings
Ingredients

- 1 cup dried red kidney beans, soaked overnight and drained
- 1 tbsp bourbon
- 1 tbsp maple syrup
- 1 onion, chopped
- 1 tbsp tomato puree
- 1 tbsp grated ginger
- 3 cups water
- 1 garlic clove, minced
- 1 slices bacon, chopped
- 1 tbsp honey mustard
- Salt

Cooking Directions

1. Add soaked and drain beans in pressure cooker.

2. Add the remaining ingredients except the salt and mix well until combine.
3. Sealed with lid and place over the high heat. When it reaches high, reduce the heat and cook for 34 minutes.
4. Remove the cooker from heat. Release the pressure through natural release method.
5. Open lid and cool completely. Store in airtight container for 5 days in refrigerator.

**Nutritional Value (Amount per Serving):** Calories **47** kcal, Total Fat **0.7** g, Carbohydrate **9** g, Protein **0.5**g, Sodium **66** mg.

# 25-Pressure Cooker Healthy Oatmeal

Total Time: 25 minutes
Serves: 4 Servings
Ingredients

- 3 cups water
- 2 cups oats
- 3 cups almond milk
- 1/2 tsp vanilla extract
- 1/2 cup dried cranberries, raisins and cherries
- 2 tbsp butter
- 1/4 tsp ground cinnamon

Cooking Directions

1. Add all the ingredients in the pressure cooker. Mix well.

2. Sealed with the lid and place over high heat. When it reaches high pressure, reduce the heat and cook for 8 minutes.
3. Remove the cooker from the heat. Release pressure through natural release method.
4. Open a lid the mixture should be creamy and loose.
5. Serve warm and enjoy.

**Nutritional Value (Amount per Serving):** Calories **629** kcal, Total Fat **51** g, Carbohydrate **39** g, Protein **9**g, Sodium **76** mg.

# 26-Simple Healthy Yellow Rice

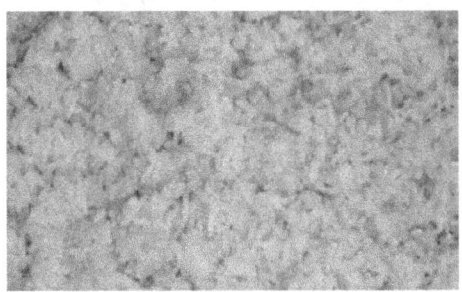

Total Time: 25 minutes
Serves: 6 Servings
Ingredients

- 2 cups small grains rice
- 1/2 cup moong dhal
- 1 tbsp butter
- 2 cups vegetable stock
- 2 tbsp chopped fresh cilantro
- 1 tbsp olive oil
- 1 tsp turmeric
- 2 pinches salt

Cooking Directions

1. Rinse the rice and moong dhal. Drained.
2. In a pressure cooker, heat the oil and butter over medium heat. Add the turmeric and sit for 20 seconds.

3. Add rice and moong dhal in cooker and mix well until well coated.
4. Add salt and vegetable stock mix well.
5. Sealed with lid and place over high heat. When it reaches high pressure, reduce the heat and cook for 5 minutes.
6. Release the pressure through natural release method.
7. Open the lid. Transfer rice in serving bowl and garnish with freshly chopped cilantro.
8. Serve hot and enjoy.

**Nutritional Value (Amount per Serving):** Calories **38** kcal, Total Fat **4** g, Carbohydrate **0.1** g, Protein **0.9**g, Sodium **64** mg.

# 27-Pressure Cooker Potato and Onion Soup

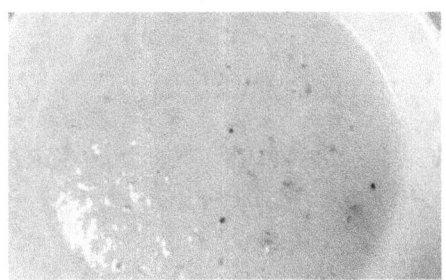

Total Time: 35 minutes
Serves: 2 Servings
Ingredients

- 2 cups vegetable stock
- 2 cups potatoes, cut into chunks
- 2 tablespoons oil
- 3 onions, sliced

Cooking Directions

1. Heat the oil in a pressure cooker over medium heat.
2. Add the onions and cook for until onions are caramelizing for 20 minutes over medium heat.
3. After onions become brown add the potatoes. Mix well and cook for about 5 minutes.
4. Add vegetable stock and sealed with the lid and place over the high heat for 5 minutes.

5. Release the pressure through natural release method.
6. Open the lid and blend soup until get desired consistency.
7. Serve hot with crusty bread.

**Nutritional Value (Amount per Serving):** Calories **290** kcal, Total Fat **13** g, Carbohydrate **39** g, Protein **4**g, Sodium **16** mg.

# 28-Pressure Cooker Quick Pork

Total Time: 40 minutes
Serves: 2 Servings
Ingredients

- 1 tbsp olive oil
- 3 oz apple juice
- 1 tsp fennel seed
- 3 oz pork tenderloins
- 8 oz sauerkraut, drained
- 1 cup water
- 6 potatoes, halved

Cooking Directions

1. Heat olive oil in a pressure cooker over medium heat.
2. Add pork tenderloins in the hot oil and stir until brown, about 5 minutes each side.

3. Add sauerkraut around the pieces of pork and add the apple juice and water. Sprinkle fennel seeds over pork.
4. Sealed with lid and cook for 15 minutes.
5. Remove cooker from heat and release the pressure through quick release method.
6. Add potatoes into cooker and resealed with lid and bring over the medium heat and cook for 7 minutes.
7. Remove the lid and serve hot.

**Nutritional Value (Amount per Serving):** Calories **631** kcal, Total Fat **11** g, Carbohydrate **110** g, Protein **24**g, Sodium **821** mg.

# 29-Pressure Cooker Roasted Turkey Legs

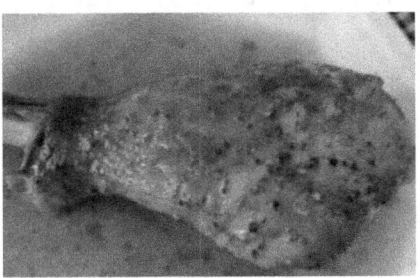

Total Time: 45 minutes
Serves: 4 Servings
Ingredients

- 4 turkey legs
- 2 tsp chicken granules
- 2 cups BBQ sauce
- 4 cups warm water

Cooking Directions

1. Place the turkey legs into pressure cooker over medium heat. Pour enough water to cover them.
2. Sprinkle chicken granules over water, and mix well.
3. Sealed with lid and place over high heat and cook for 5 minutes.
4. While turkey is cooking, preheat ovens broiler.
5. Remove cooker from heat and release the pressure.

6. Remove the lid and place turkey legs on roasting tray.
7. Roast the turkey legs for 15 minutes, until it crispy and brown.
8. Rub the BBQ sauce over the roasted turkey legs and serve.

**Nutritional Value (Amount per Serving):** Calories **188** kcal, Total Fat **0.4** g, Carbohydrate **45** g, Protein **0.1**g, Sodium **1406** mg.

# 30-Pressure Cooker Chicken Stock

Total Time: 40 minutes

Serves: 8 Servings
Ingredients

- 1 onion, diced in 4 pieces
- 1 large carrot, cut into 4 pieces
- 1 stalk celery, cut into 4 pieces
- 1 chicken carcass
- 5 cloves garlic
- 7 black peppercorns
- 2 liter water
- 1 tsp salt, to taste

Cooking Directions

1. Add carrots, onion, celery, garlic cloves, chicken carcass and peppercorns into a pressure cooker.
2. Add water and seal with the lid.
3. Place cooker over high heat. Reduce the heat and cook for 30 minutes.

4. Remove cooker from the heat and release pressure through natural release method.
5. Open the lid and strain the stock into bowl.
6. Let the stock cool completely and then place in refrigerator.

**Nutritional Value (Amount per Serving):** Calories **13** kcal, Total Fat **0.1** g, Carbohydrate **2.9** g, Protein **0.4**g, Sodium **307** mg.

# 31-Pressure Cooker Chicken Stew

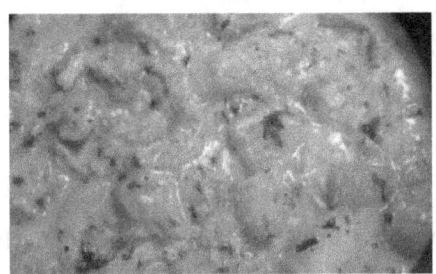

Total Time: 60 minutes
Serves: 4 Servings
Ingredients

- 900g whole chicken
- 2 habanera peppers, minced
- 1 small onion, chopped
- 1/2 tsp ground cumin
- 1 garlic clove, minced
- 2 carrots, chopped
- 3 stalks celery, chopped
- 3 fresh chopped tomatoes
- 1/2 tsp dried thyme
- 1 tbsp dried basil
- 2 oz can green chili peppers, chopped
- 1 potato, diced
- 1 1/2 tbsp all-purpose flour
- Pepper
- Salt to taste

Cooking Directions

1. Add the chicken in cooker add water to cover place cooker over medium heat.
2. Add the thyme, cumin and basil. Sealed with lid.
3. Bring to boil, reduce heat and cook for 40 minutes.
4. Remove the chicken from cooker and allow it to cool.
5. Remove bones and skin and chop chicken into small pieces.
6. Return the chicken into the cooker and add green chili peppers, garlic, onions, carrots, celery, potatoes, habanerapepper and tomatoes.
7. Resealed with lid and cook for 10 minutes.
8. Open the lid. In a small bowl, add flour with little water and add in the stew.
9. Increase heat for minute and stir well.
10. Season with pepper and salt to taste and serve hot.

**Nutritional Value (Amount per Serving):** Calories **521** kcal, Total Fat **17** g, Carbohydrate **20** g, Protein **68**g, Sodium **274** mg.

# 32-Pressure Cooker BBQ Ribs

Total Time: 60 minutes
Serves: 4 Servings
Ingredients

- 1 cup BBQ sauce
- 5 cloves
- 1 onion, diced
- 1/2 cup water
- 1/2 cup apple jelly
- 1  cinnamon stick
- 1200g pork ribs

Cooking Directions

1. Add all ingredients in pressure cooker expect pork ribs and mix well until combined.
2. Add pork ribs in mixture mix well until all are coated well.

3. Sealed with the lid and place over low heat and cook for 45 minutes.
4. Release pressure through natural release method and open the lid.
5. Remove the bones, cloves and cinnamon stick from pressure cooker.
6. Return cooker over medium heat and cook for 15 minutes.
7. Serve hot and enjoy.

**Nutritional Value (Amount per Serving):** Calories **1000** kcal, Total Fat **53** g, Carbohydrate **52** g, Protein **89**g, Sodium **888** mg.

# 33-Pressure Cooker Mashed Turnip

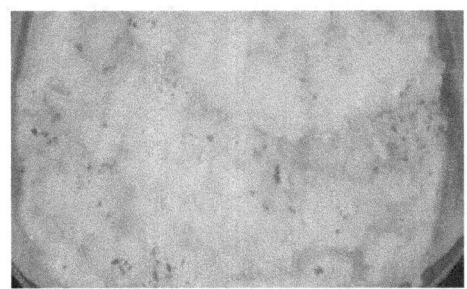

Total Time: 20 minutes
Serves: 4 Servings
Ingredients

- 4 turnips, diced
- 1 onion, chopped
- 1/2 cup chicken stock
- 1/4 cup sour cream
- Black pepper
- Salt to taste

Cooking Directions

1. Add turnip, chopped onion and chicken stock in pressure cooker sealed with lid and place over the high heat for 5 minutes.
2. Release the pressure through natural release method.
3. Drain the turnip and blend until get smooth puree.

4. Add sour cream and mix well. Season with pepper and salt to taste.

**Nutritional Value (Amount per Serving):** Calories **78** kcal, Total Fat **3** g, Carbohydrate **11** g, Protein **1**g, Sodium **223** mg.

# 34-Pressure Cooker Carrot Puree

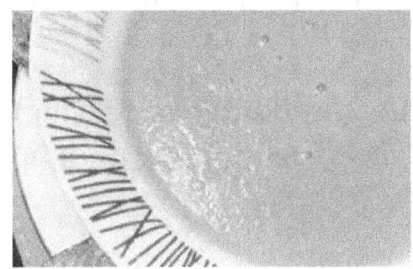

Total Time: 20 minutes
Serves: 4 Servings
Ingredients

- 3 carrots, cut into 2 inch pieces
- 2 turnips, cut into 4 pieces
- 1 cup water
- 1 tbsp oil
- 1/4 tsp grated nutmeg
- 1 tbsp sour cream
- 1/2 tsp salt

Cooking Directions

1. Add carrots, turnips, water and salt in pressure cooker and sealed with lid and place over the high heat for 10 minutes.
2. Release the pressure and drain the vegetables.

3. Blend the vegetables until get smooth puree or you desired consistency.
4. Add the grated nutmeg, sour cream and salt to taste mix well.

**Nutritional Value (Amount per Serving):** Calories **73** kcal, Total Fat **4** g, Carbohydrate **8** g, Protein **1**g, Sodium **363** mg.

# 35-Pressure Cooker Shrimp Rice

Total Time: 20 minutes
Serves: 4 Servings
Ingredients

- 2 tbsp oil
- 2 tbsp tomato puree
- 3 cup chicken stock
- 450g shrimp
- 1 onion, diced
- 1 tsp fennel seeds
- 3 garlic cloves, minced
- 1 1/2 cup rice
- Black pepper
- Salt

Cooking Directions

1. In a pressure cooker add olive oil over medium heat; add fennel seed and onion and sauté until onion soften.
2. Add garlic, tomato puree rice and mix well. Add chicken stock.
3. Sealed with lid and place over the high heat for 6 minutes.
4. Release the pressure and open the lid.
5. Add shrimp and simmer for 3 minutes until shrimp are cooked.
6. Season with pepper and salt.
7. Serve hot immediately.

**Nutritional Value (Amount per Serving):** Calories **473** kcal, Total Fat **9** g, Carbohydrate **62** g, Protein **31**g, Sodium **897** mg.

# 36-Pressure Cooker Vegetable Broth

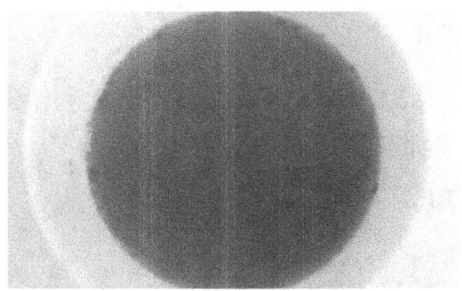

Total Time: 25 minutes
Serves: 4 Servings
Ingredients

- 4 cups water
- 1 bay leaf
- 10 peppercorns
- 4 garlic cloves
- 3 stalks celery, cut into half
- 2 carrots, cut into pieces
- 2 onion, diced

Cooking Directions

1. Add all ingredients in pressure cooker and sealed with lid and place over the medium heat for 10 minutes.

2. Release the pressure through natural release method and strain the stock through strainer.
3. Pour the stock in airtight container and stored in refrigerator.

**Nutritional Value (Amount per Serving):** Calories **42** kcal, Total Fat **0.9** g, Carbohydrate **9** g, Protein **1**g, Sodium **41** mg.

# 37-Pressure Cooker Mushroom Broth

Total Time: 20 minutes
Serves: 4 Servings
Ingredients

- 4 cup water
- 1 cup mushroom, sliced
- Pinch of chili flakes
- 2 whole cloves
- 1/2 celery stalk, chopped
- 1 onion, diced
- 1 leeks, cleaned and cut into pieces
- 2 carrots, cut into large pieces

Cooking Directions

1. Add all ingredients in pressure cooker and sealed with lid and place over the low heat for 15 minutes.
2. Release the heat through natural release method.

3. Remove the lid and strain the stock through strainer.
4. Pour stock in airtight container and stored in refrigerator.

**Nutritional Value (Amount per Serving):** Calories **41** kcal, Total Fat **0.2** g, Carbohydrate **9** g, Protein **1.4**g, Sodium **36** mg.

## 38-Pressure Cooker Fish Stock

Total Time: 20 minutes
Serves: 4 Servings
Ingredients

- 4 cup water
- 1/2 onion, diced
- 1 small carrot, diced
- 1 stalks celery, cut into half
- 3 black peppercorns
- 450g fish heads and bones

Cooking Directions

1. Add all ingredients in pressure cooker and sealed with lid and place over the medium-high heat for 15 minutes.
2. Release the heat through natural release method.

3. Remove the lid and strain the stock through strainer.
4. Pour stock in airtight container and stored in refrigerator for 2 months.

**Nutritional Value (Amount per Serving):** Calories **12** kcal, Total Fat **0.2** g, Carbohydrate **2** g, Protein **0.4**g, Sodium **20** mg.

# 39-Yellow Split Pea and Red Lentil Soup

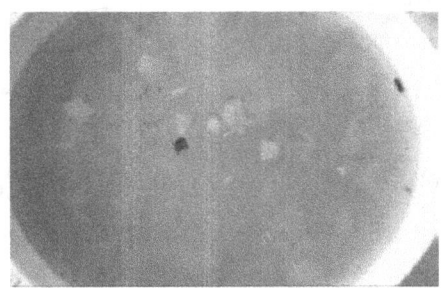

Total Time: 35 minutes
Serves: 5 Servings
Ingredients

- 1/2 cup red lentils
- 2 cloves garlic, minced
- 1 tsp ground cumin
- 4 cups chicken stock
- 1/2 cup yellow split peas
- 1/2 onion, sliced
- 1 carrots, chopped
- 1 tsp lemon juice
- Black pepper
- Salt to taste

Cooking Directions

1. Add lentils, split peas, carrots, onion, garlic and cumin into the pressure cooker.

2. Pour the chicken stock in pressure cooker.
3. Seal the cooker with lid and place cooker over medium heat.
4. Reduce heat and cook for 30 minutes.
5. Remove cooker from heat, release the pressure and open the lid.
6. Season with pepper and salt and add lemon juice stir once and serve.

**Nutritional Value (Amount per Serving):** Calories **156** kcal, Total Fat **1** g, Carbohydrate **26** g, Protein **10**g, Sodium **656** mg.

# 40-Pressure Cooker Mango Jam

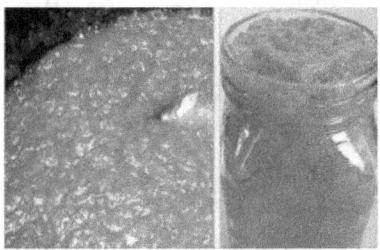

Total Time: 25 minutes
Serves: 2 Servings
Ingredients

- 2 ripe mangoes, chopped
- 2 tsp mustard powder
- 1 cup vinegar
- 3/4 cup sugar
- 3/4 cup brown sugar
- 6 dried plums, chopped
- 2 tsp grated ginger
- 1 garlic clove
- 2 jalapeno peppers, minced
- Pinch of salt

Cooking Directions

1. Add all ingredients in pressure cooker and sealed with lid and place over the high heat for 8 minutes.

2. Release the heat through quick release method. Remove the lid.
3. Return the pressure cooker over medium heat for 10 minutes.
4. Cover the jam and refrigerate for overnight before using.

**Nutritional Value (Amount per Serving):** Calories **543** kcal, Total Fat **1** g, Carbohydrate **133** g, Protein **1**g, Sodium **467** mg.

Conclusion

A healthy diet is now achievable and preparing it in so many ways will make it enticing as you try a diversity of flavors. Pressurized cookers have proven its asset in making the best and richly flavoured recipes that one can experience. Meals without the hassle but is chef-like in nature and taste is a win-win situation. Enjoy the experience with your family, relatives and friends -at all time and all occasions! Start working on a recipe now and make every bite worth it!

# Part 2

# Introduction

What is a Pressure Cooker?

A pressure cooker is a covered pot that is placed on the stove to help cook food quickly, without losing the essential vitamins and minerals that it contains. When the pot is covered with the lid, the heat begins to create steam and this quickly raises the temperature in the pot.

As the steam builds, so does the pressure which allows you to cook foods approximately 70% faster than traditional methods. Additionally, food is tender with this cooking approach, because of the liquid that is used for the cooking process.

New pressure cookers have a safety device on them that allows the stem to be vented without causing an explosion on the stove. The lid of the cooker also cannot be opened due to a locking mechanism until you have reduced the pressure of the pot, often by running cold water over the top.

What are the Benefits of Pressure Cooking?

Knowing what a pressure cooker can do, what are the benefits of pressure cooking?

To begin with, this form of cooking saves time for busy families. You can stick an entire meal in the pressure cooker and save a great deal cooking time. Just throw in some meat, rice and some vegetables, and in under 30 minutes it is possible to have a complete meal you can serve your family without a lot of prep work.

In the summer, pressure cookers will also help to keep the room cooler. Since less heat is being generated while using them, it will have a minimal impact on the temperature in your home, as compared to using an oven or having several pots boiling or a frying pan on the stove.

It will also save you money. Since cooking takes place in a fraction of the time, you are using less electricity or gas to cook the meal. That will mean lower energy bills and more money in your pocket. Those savings can be taken a step further by choosing cheaper cuts of meat which tend to be tougher. The pressure cooker will help to tenderize the meat so you don't have to worry about buying choice cuts of meat.

When you fry and bake foods, many of the nutrients in the dish are cooked out. That means you lose a lot of the nutritional value. When you focus on pressure cooking your foods, more nutrients are maintained and that means the food that you are serving your family is actually better for them.

Since food can be cooked in almost no time, you can also put an end to high calorie and fat fast food meals. Once sought after thanks to the convenience, you can enjoy a nutritionally rich meal in under 30 minutes. That is about the time it takes to drive out of your way to get fast food, sit in line and wait for it to be cooked by someone else.

When you take into account the cost per person when you make a meal in a pressure cooker compared to what you spend at the fast food joint, you are actually saving money in the process as well.

Cleanup is even easier with a pressure cooker. Since many meals can be prepared in a single cooker, you will only have the unit to clean. Just wash it out, dry it and it will be ready for the next meal you make. It doesn't get any easier than that.

Types of Pressure Cookers

There are essentially two different types of pressure cookers. The first is the conventional pressure cooker. This is the cooker that is placed on the stove that uses either an electric or gas burner to build up the steam pressure inside of it for cooking. This tends to go quickly and will help you to cook faster.

The maximum pressure that these stovetop variations can reach is 15 PSI. All the recipe directions in my book follow conventional pressure cooking methods.

The second type of pressure cooker is the electric pressure cooker. This tends to cook slower, as it takes more time for the pressure to build in the system. While you do need to monitor the stovetop cooker, the electric pressure cooker will require no monitoring and it will release and maintain the pressure for you, based on the settings.

Typically, these cookers have an internal heating source, so that less heat enters the kitchen. The maximum PSI for these units can vary. Some will only reach a low setting of 8 PSI while others might hit 15 PSI.

How to Use a Pressure Cooker

Using a pressure cooker isn't too complicated. There are a few simple things to keep in mind. Typically, low pressure cooking takes place at 8 PSI. In turn, high pressure cooking is 15 PSI.

Before using a pressure cooker, ensure you review the owner's manual and ensure that you have all the parts that are necessary for cooking. Never use a pressure cooker that is damaged, cracked, dented or missing safety parts.

For Electric Pressure Cookers: There is no standard for these pressure cookers. Typically, there is a brown setting that is used for the initial browning, typically for meat. You can then select the pressure setting and the cooking time you'd like to have.

Never use cold water released on this type of pressure cooker and keep your hand clear of escaping steam. Press the quick release mechanism to ensure that the pressure safely drops.

Prior to cooking anything in the pressure cooker, you need to add some liquid into the pot. Typically, this is water but broth or other liquids can also be used. For old fashioned pressure cookers, you'll need to add at least a cup of liquid, while modern pressure cookers will need only 1/2 a cup of water to properly cook.

When adding liquid, never fill it more than 2/3 of the way full with water and food. If cooking beans or foods that will foam or froth, do not fill it more than halfway.

Once you have your pot filled, you'll want to set the heat to medium high on your stove. Using high heat can actually cause problems for the pressure cooker. After 3 – 5 minutes, you should start to notice the pressure building in the unit. As soon as the pressure has built, it is important to not attempt to open the top until you have lowered the pressure.

Adjust the heat beneath the cooker as needed to help the pot reach the proper PSI for the recipe that you are making. As soon as the appropriate cooking time has elapsed, take the pressure cooker off the stove and release the pressure. You can do a natural release which takes some time, use the pressure release on the device that can slowly reduce pressure, or you can run cool water over the top of a conventional pressure cooker.

Here are a few tips to remember:
- To ensure you create the best meal possible, soak beans overnight to soften them up.
- Meat should be browned in advance to help seal in the juices and flavor.
- When possible, cook vegetables last to help avoid a mushy mess in the food.
- If you begin to see steam coming out from the sides or it is spraying liquid, your pressure cooker is too high. Turn down the temperature or remove it from the stove. Ignoring the buildup of pressure can cause the top of older pressure cookers to explode.

And now, on to the recipes! Each delicious meal won't take long to prepare and your entire family will love. Before you know it, you will have mastered the art of cooking with a pressure cooker, leaving you more time to spend with your family.

# Pressure Cooker Recipes

Sweet and Sour Chicken Breasts

If you love the tangy sweet flavor of sweet and sour sauce, you will love this delicious dish.

Ingredients:
- 6 boneless, skinless chicken breast halves (approximately 2 1/2- 3 lbs.)
- 1 can pineapple chunks (20 oz., + 1 cup pineapple juice)
- 1/2 cup bell pepper (chopped)
- 1/2 cup celery (chopped)
- 1/2 cup vinegar
- 1/4 cup brown sugar
- 2 tablespoons water
- 2 tablespoons cornstarch
- 2 tablespoons soy sauce

- 1 tablespoon ketchup
- 1 tablespoon olive oil
- 1/2 teaspoon Worcestershire sauce
- 1/4 teaspoon ginger (ground)

Directions:

Brown chicken in olive oil in the bottom of the pressure cooker over medium high heat. Add the bell pepper and celery. Whisk the vinegar, brown sugar, soy sauce, ketchup, Worcestershire sauce, pineapple juice and ginger in a bowl and pour over the chicken and vegetables.

Seal the lid and bring to full pressure and cook for 8 minutes. Cool rapidly. Remove chicken and vegetables and mix the water and cornstarch and add to the liquid in the pressure cooker. Turn heat to high and boil until thickened. Stir in pineapple chunks and chicken and vegetables and heat thoroughly.

Serves: 6

# Rice 'N Tips

A savory favorite that is light and filling. It is great alone or served with a tossed salad.

Ingredients:
- 4 cups beef (cubed sirloin)
- 1 can beef consommé (10.5 oz.)
- 4 cups brown rice (cooked)
- 1 cup onion (chopped)
- 3 tablespoons flour (all-purpose)
- 2 tablespoons olive oil
- 2 teaspoons salt
- 1 teaspoon garlic (minced)
- 1/2 teaspoon paprika
- 1/2 teaspoon pepper
- 1/4 teaspoon mustard powder

Directions:

In a bowl, mix together the flour, salt, paprika, pepper, and mustard powder and spread over beef. Brown the beef in the oil in the bottom of the cooker. Stir in the onion and garlic. Pour in the beef consommé. Cook until onion is tender. Seal the cooker and turn heat to medium for 25 minutes. Depressurize and continue to heat and stir until the sauce thickens. Serve over hot cooked brown rice.

Serves: 6

# Barbecue Ribs

This delicious dish can be made with either pork or beef ribs.

Ingredients:
- 5 lbs. boneless ribs (beef or pork)
- 2 cups ketchup
- 2 cups onions (chopped)
- 1/2 cup apple cider vinegar
- 1/2 cup vinegar
- 3 teaspoons olive oil
- 2 teaspoons Worcestershire sauce
- 1 teaspoon celery seed
- 1 teaspoon chili powder
- 1 teaspoon garlic powder
- 1/8 – 1/4 teaspoon paprika
- Salt and pepper

Directions:

Add garlic powder, paprika, salt and pepper over the ribs. Turn the heat to medium high and brown the ribs in the olive oil in the bottom of the pressure cooker. On top of the ribs, add ketchup, onions, apple cider, vinegar, Worcestershire sauce, celery seed, and chili powder. Seal the lid and cook on medium high until it reaches full pressure. Cook for 15 minutes. Allow pressure to release and serve hot.

Serves: 8

# Cheesy Mushrooms and Rice

This classic "mushroom risotto" is a favorite for a light lunch or a main dish for supper.

Ingredients:
- 4 cups chicken stock
- 3 cups portabella mushrooms (sliced)
- 1 1/2 cups risotto rice
- 1 1/4 cups Parmesan cheese (grated)
- 1/2 cup of onion (chopped)
- 4 tablespoons butter
- 4 tablespoons extra virgin olive oil
- 1 teaspoon of garlic (minced)

Directions:

Sauté the onions and garlic in extra virgin olive oil and 2 tablespoons of butter in the bottom of the pressure cooker over medium high heat. Stir in the portabella mushrooms and risotto rice. Stir in the chicken stock. Seal the lid and bring to pressure over medium high heat for at least 7 minutes. Release the pressure, remove the lid and stir in the remaining 2 tablespoons of butter and the Parmesan cheese. Serve hot.

Serves: 6

# Chicken and Sausage Delight

This is a tasty dish combining Italian sausage with chicken breast and delicious bell peppers.

Ingredients:
- 1 3/4 lbs. Italian sausage
- 4 chicken breast halves (boneless, skinless)
- 1 can tomatoes (16 oz. can, diced)
- 1 cup bell peppers (1 red, 1 green)
- 1/2 cup onion (chopped)
- 2 tablespoons red wine vinegar
- 1 tablespoon olive oil
- 1 teaspoon garlic (minced)
- 3/4 teaspoon basil (dried)
- 1/4 teaspoon fennel seed
- 1/8 teaspoon red pepper flakes
- Salt and black pepper

Directions:

Cook the sausage and chicken in the oil in the cooker until browned. Remove from cooker. Add the peppers, onion, and garlic and sauté. Add the meat, vinegar, basil, fennel seed, and dashes of salt, black pepper, and red pepper flakes. Seal the cooker and turn up to medium high heat. Reduce heat when pressure is full and cook for about 10 minutes.

Serves: 6-8

# Chicken Noodles

This is a delicious comfort food dish that the whole family will love.

Ingredients:
- 3 lbs. chicken breast tenders (boneless, skinless)
- 6 oz. egg noodles (cooked)
- 3-4 cups tomato (chopped)
- 1/2 cup chicken stock
- 1/2 cup onion (chopped)
- 1/2 cup sour cream
- 1 tablespoon olive oil
- 2 teaspoons paprika
- 1 teaspoon salt

Directions:

Cook the chicken in the oil in the bottom of the pressure cooker for 4 minutes. Remove chicken. Add in chicken stock, onion, and paprika and whisk together. Add the chicken with the tomatoes and salt. Seal the lid and cook on high for 4 minutes. Cook on medium heat for 7 minutes, turn heat off and leave for 3 minutes. Remove the chicken. While stirring with a whisk, add the sour cream to the liquid. Add the chicken and reheat. Serve over noodles.

Serves: 4

# Chicken and Salad

Sometimes you just need a good salad with some seasoned chicken to make a great meal.

Ingredients:
- 2 lbs. chicken breast (boneless, skinless)
- 1 1/2 cups chicken stock
- 2 tablespoons extra virgin olive oil
- Salt and pepper
- Tossed salad for 6
- Dressing to taste

Directions:

Rinse the chicken breasts. Liberally sprinkle salt and pepper over all sides of the chicken. Brown the chicken in the olive oil in the bottom of the pressure cooker. Pour the chicken stock in the cooker. Seal the lid and turn the heat to medium high to bring up to full pressure. Cook for about 25 minutes. Release the pressure and allow the chicken to cool for a few minutes. Cut into bite sizes and serve on top of the tossed salad along with your favorite salad dressing.

Serves: 6

# Jambalaya

This dish is for when nothing but Cajun food will hit the spot.

Ingredients:
- 8 oz. shrimp (peeled, deveined, uncooked)
- 1 can tomatoes (14.5 oz., diced, undrained)
- 1 cup Andouille sausage (sliced)
- 1 cup chicken breasts (chopped)
- 1 cup chicken stock
- 1 cup long-grain rice
- 3/4 cup celery (chopped)
- 1/2 cup bell pepper (chopped)
- 1/2 cup onion (chopped)
- 1/2 tablespoon olive oil
- 3 teaspoons parsley (dried)
- 2 teaspoons Cajun seasoning
- 1 1/2 teaspoons garlic (minced)
- 1 teaspoon thyme (dried)
- 1/2 teaspoon cayenne pepper (or adjusted to your taste)
- 1/8 teaspoon hot sauce (or adjusted to your taste)

Directions:

Brown the shrimp, sausage, and chicken in the olive oil in the bottom of the pressure cooker. During browning add 1 teaspoon Cajun seasoning, hot sauce, and thyme.

Remove the meat and add the remaining spices along with the vegetables and rice. Seal the lid and cook over medium high heat for 8 minutes at full pressure. Add the meat and continue to stir and cook for another 5 minutes.

Serves: 4

# Pintos and Ham

A southern favorite, a bowl of pintos and ham is delicious with a slice of hot cornbread. Try this flavorful comfort food any time of year, particularly when the weather is cold outside. The leftovers taste even better.

Ingredients:
- 1 lb. pinto beans (dried, soaked overnight)
- 6 cups water (hot)
- 2 cups ham (cubed)
- 1/2 cup onion (chopped)
- 1 tablespoon olive oil
- 1/2 teaspoon garlic (minced)
- Salt and pepper

Directions:

Sauté the onions and garlic in olive oil in the bottom of the pressure cooker over medium heat. Add the beans, ham, and dashes of salt and pepper. Seal the lid and cook on medium high heat until it reaches pressure. Turn to low heat and cook an additional half an hour. Test the beans for tenderness and continue to pressure cook in 5 minute increments until they are tender.

Serves: 8

# Pork Chops with Potatoes and Carrots

Serve a meal with meat and potatoes from one pot.

Ingredients:
- 6 thick pork chops (approximately 2 1/2 -3 pounds)
- 6 russet potatoes (peeled, chopped)
- 1 1/2 cups carrots (chopped)
- 1 1/2 cups vegetable stock
- 1 cup onion (chopped)
- 1/3 cup butter
- 4 1/2 tablespoons Worcestershire sauce
- Salt and Pepper

Directions:

First, sprinkle salt and pepper over both sides of the pork chops. Next, add 3 tablespoons of butter into the pressure cooker and turn heat to medium-high. Brown the pork chops and set aside. Add the remaining butter to the pressure cooker along with the carrots and onions and sauté. Pour in the vegetable stock and Worcestershire sauce. Return the pork chops to the pressure cooker and place the potatoes and carrots on top. Seal the lid and cook for 12 minutes.

Serves: 6

# Seasoned Cabbage

This is a delicious dish that reminds us of the wonderful southern-cooked dishes. Serve alone or with your favorite bread and potato dish.

Ingredients:
- 1/2 pound smoked sausage (sliced)
- 2 tablespoons olive oil
- 1 head cabbage, chopped
- 2 cups chicken stock
- 1/4 cup butter
- Salt and pepper

Directions:

Cook the sliced smoked sausage in a skillet in the olive oil. Meanwhile, add the chopped cabbage to the pressure cooker along with the chicken stock. Set the heat on high until full pressure is reached and turn to low and cook for about three minutes. Remove pot from heat and release the pressure. Toss in a serving bowl with the cooked sausage and dashes of salt and pepper.

Serves: 6

# Spicy Rice Pilaf

Bean sprouts make this dish a little different, and added with a bit of spiciness, it makes for a delightful main dish.

Ingredients:
- 2 1/2 cups hot water
- 1 cup bean sprouts
- 1 cup rice (long grain, soaked for 10 minutes)
- 1/2 cup onions (chopped)
- 1 teaspoon coriander seeds (ground)
- 1 teaspoon olive oil
- 1 teaspoon red chili powder
- 1/2 teaspoon cumin seeds
- 1/2 teaspoon ginger (ground)
- 1/2 teaspoon green chili paste
- 1/4 teaspoon turmeric powder
- 1/8 teaspoon ground cinnamon
- 1/8 teaspoon ground clove
- Salt to taste

Directions:

Sauté the onions, cumin seeds, ginger, green chili paste, cloves, and cinnamon in the olive oil in the pressure cooker over medium high heat. Stir in the bean sprouts and rice, and cook for 2-3 minutes. Add the water, coriander seeds, red chili powder, and turmeric along with dashes of salt. Seal the lid and bring to high pressure for 15 minutes.

Serves: 4

# Split Pea Soup

This delicious and nutritious bowl of comfort food is best served with a hot corn muffin. This is perfect for cold days.

Ingredients:
- 1 lb. bag split peas (dried and soaked overnight)
- 6 cups beef stock
- 2 cups ham (cubed)
- 2 cups potatoes (chopped)
- 1 cup onions (chopped)
- 1/2 cup carrots (chopped)
- 1/2 cup celery (chopped)
- 1/4 teaspoon thyme (dried)
- Salt and pepper

Directions:

Drain the peas and add to the pressure cooker along with the onions, carrots, celery, thyme, and salt and pepper (to taste). Turn heat to medium high and bring to full pressure for about 20 minutes. Allow release of steam to occur slowly. Taste and add more salt and pepper if needed. Add ham, potatoes, and carrots and bring to pressure again for about 10 minutes. Serve with cornbread or corn muffins.

Serves: 8

# Tender Chicken and Vegetables

A delicious hot chicken and vegetable meal.

Ingredients:
- 4 boneless, skinless chicken breast halves (approximately 1 1/2 – 2 lbs.)
- 2 cups tomatoes (crushed)
- 1 1/2 cups onions (chopped)
- 1 cup mushrooms (chopped)
- 1/2 cup bell pepper (chopped)
- 1/2 cup Parmesan cheese (grated)
- 1/2 cup white wine
- 1/4 cup black olives (pitted, sliced)
- 2 tablespoons tomato paste
- 1 tablespoon olive oil
- 1 1/2 teaspoons garlic (minced)
- Salt and pepper

Directions:

Cook the onions and peppers in olive oil until tender. Add the white wine and stir until it cooks down to half. Add the chopped mushrooms, garlic and chicken. Pour the crushed tomatoes over the chicken. Add the tomato paste on the very top. Seal the lid and cook for just under 10 minutes. Allow to depressurize slowly. Add the olives, Parmesan cheese, and salt and pepper to taste.

Serves: 4

# Blissful Beef Stew

After a long day at work, nothing is more relaxing than a piping hot bowl of beef stew. Chock full of flavorful ingredients, this easy-to-make meal will have you warmed up in minutes.

Ingredients:
- 1.5 pounds stew meat (cubed)
- 2 cups beef broth
- 5 carrots (sliced thin)
- 1 medium onion (diced)
- 2 cloves garlic (minced)
- 4 potatoes (peeled and chopped)
- 3 stalks of celery (sliced)
- 1 can diced tomatoes (14.5 oz. can)

- 1 tablespoon Worcestershire
- 2 tablespoons vegetable oil
- ¼ cup flour
- Salt and pepper to taste

Directions:

Heat oil over medium heat. Coat beef cubes with flour and place in oil until well browned, turning often. Add broth, Worcestershire, and onion to beef and bring to a boil. Bring to high pressure by closing cover. Cook on high pressure for 15 minutes. Remove from heat and take to low pressure; remove cover. Add remaining vegetables and seasonings to taste. Cover and return to high pressure for 5 minutes. Turn off and remove from heat. Remove cover, stir gently, and serve with warm rolls or biscuits.

Serves: 6

# Pleasantly Pleasing Pork Ribs

Ribs are great any time of the year, but frequently skipped over because traditional cooking requires several hours of cooking time. A pressure cooker will have these tasty tidbits ready for you and your family in under 30 minutes.

Ingredients:
- 2 pounds country-style pork ribs (boneless)
- 1 tablespoon olive oil
- 1 cup water
- 4 teaspoons white vinegar
- 1 teaspoon Worcestershire
- 1 teaspoon onion salt
- 1 teaspoon pepper
- 1 teaspoon paprika
- 1 teaspoon prepared mustard
- 3 tablespoons ketchup

Directions:

Sprinkle ribs with paprika, pepper, and salt. Place oil and ribs in pressure cooker and brown all sides. Remove and drain. Place meat back in cooker and add remaining ingredients. Bring to high pressure, and reduce to medium-high pressure. Cook for 15 minutes. Remove from heat and let pressure drop naturally.

Remove fat and spoon sauce over ribs. Serve with rice or baked potatoes.

Serves: 4

# Mexicana Tamale Surprise

Your family can still enjoy the tamales they love when you change the traditional cornmeal wrap to a cabbage leaf. Freeze leftovers and reheat in the microwave for another meal.

Ingredients:
- 1 1/2 cups white rice (uncooked)
- 16 oz. can tomato sauce
- 1 lb. ground beef
- 8 cabbage leaves (large)
- 1/4 cup onion (diced)
- 1/2 cup green pepper (deseeded and diced)
- 2 teaspoons red chili powder
- 2 cans diced tomatoes (10 oz. cans)
- 2 cloves garlic (minced)
- Salt and black pepper to taste

Directions:

Soften the cabbage leaves by boiling them for 3 minutes. Remove and put on a paper towel. Combine the rice, chili powder, salt, pepper, ground beef, tomato sauce, onion, and garlic in a medium bowl. Put an even amount on each cabbage leaf. Roll into tamale shapes with edges of leaf tucked underneath. Place in pressure cooker.

Cover with tomatoes and green pepper. Close pressure cooker and bring it to full pressure. Reduce heat to medium-low. Maintain full pressure and cook for 1 hour. Let the pressure reduce naturally.

Serves: 8

# Sensational Steamed Salmon

Wrapping foil around each salmon steak before cooking keeps the consistency and adds to the delicate flavor of this favorite type of fish. Enjoy the convenience of using fresh or frozen fillets.

Ingredients:
- 1 1/2 cups medium tomatoes (sliced)
- 3 salmon fillets (approximately 1 lb.)
- 1/2 cup white onion (sliced into thin rings)
- 1/2 cup lemon (sliced)
- 4-6 teaspoons olive oil
- 3 sprigs parsley
- 3 sprigs thyme
- Salt and pepper, to taste

Directions:

Tear aluminum foil into 3 sheets large enough to fasten tightly around the ingredients. Swirl 2 drops of olive oil at the foil's center. Layer the tomato slices, salt and pepper, drop of oil, fillet, salt and pepper, herbs, drop of oil, onion, and lemon. Top with drop of oil. Wrap foil into a snug packet.

Put 2 cups of water into the pressure cooker. Add steamer basket and put the salmon packets on its top. Close the cooker. Bring to full pressure. Reduce heat to low. Cook 15 minutes. Release steam, leaving lid closed. Let sit 5 minutes. Open lid and remove packets. Remove foil and serve.

Serves: 3

# Favorite Veggies and Chicken Stew

Use your favorite cuts of chicken and types of vegetables to make a warm, filling stew to chase away the chill of winter evenings.

Ingredients:
- 2 cups boneless, skinless chicken breast (cubed)
- 4 cups potatoes (peeled and chopped)
- 2/3 cup carrots (peeled and sliced)
- 1/3 cup celery (diced)
- 4 sprigs parsley
- 3 tablespoon olive oil
- 2 cups zucchini (sliced)
- 1 tablespoon thyme (dried)
- 9 tablespoons flour
- Salt and pepper to taste
- 2 cups chicken stock
- 1 garlic clove (minced)

Directions:

Heat oil in pressure cooker. Season the flour with salt and pepper to taste in medium bowl. Add chicken and stir until coated. Place chicken in oil a few pieces at a time. Stir until all sides are golden brown. Remove and set aside. Repeat until all chicken is cooked. Add in chicken, garlic, and onion into cooker and stir 3 minutes.

Add in remaining ingredients except for the stock and parsley. Cook 3 minutes. Add stock and bring to a boil. Cover cooker and bring to pressure. Reduce burner to medium–low. Cook 20 minutes. Release pressure and let pan sit 5 minutes. Remove cover. Stir. Add parsley garnish before serving.

Serves: 4

# Creamy Fresh Tomato Soup

Ward off the winter chill with delicious homemade tomato soup accompanied by rolls, biscuits, or cornbread.

Ingredients:
- 3/4 cup celery (diced)
- 3 tablespoon butter
- 1/2 cup carrots (diced)
- 1/2 cup onion (diced)
- 1 teaspoon garlic (minced)
- 2 cans chicken broth (14.5 oz. cans)
- 1/4 cup basil (fresh, chopped)
- 4 cups tomatoes (peeled, cored, and quartered)
- 1/2 teaspoon salt
- 1 tablespoon tomato paste
- 1/2 cup Parmesan cheese (shredded)
- 1 cup half & half
- 1/2 teaspoon black pepper

Directions:

Melt butter in cooker. Add celery, onions, garlic, and carrots. Sauté until tender. Add basil, stock, salt, tomatoes, tomato paste, and pepper. Seal cover and bring to pressure, reducing heat to medium. Cook 10 minutes.

Remove from burner. Reduce pressure and uncover after 5 minutes. Puree soup with immersion blender until creamy. Stir in cheese and half & half.

Serves: 6

# Wholesome Lentil Soup with Ham

Extra flavor from a ham hock complements the canned lentils in this easy- to-make, hearty meal.

Ingredients:
- 1 smoked ham hock (skin removed)
- 1 bay leaf
- 2 cups water
- 1/2 cup onion (peeled and diced)
- 3 cups chicken stock
- 1/2 cup carrots (diced)
- 1/2 cups celery (diced)
- 2 garlic cloves (peeled and minced)
- 2 cans lentils (14 oz. cans, drained)
- 1 tablespoon olive oil
- Salt and pepper to taste

Directions:

Put bay leaf, stock, ham hock, and water in pressure cooker. Bring to pressure. Cook 30 minutes. After 15 minutes has passed, heat olive oil in large saucepan over medium-low heat. Stir in garlic, carrots, onion, and celery with pinch of salt. Cook 10 minutes, stirring every two minutes. Release pressure on cooker and remove bay leaf and ham hock. Pour stock into saucepan; stir in lentils. Bring to boil. Shred ham from bone. Cut into bite sized pieces. Add to saucepan with salt and pepper to taste. Stir. Cook 2 minutes over medium high heat and serve.

Serves: 4

# Flavorful Homemade Tomato Sauce with Fettuccine

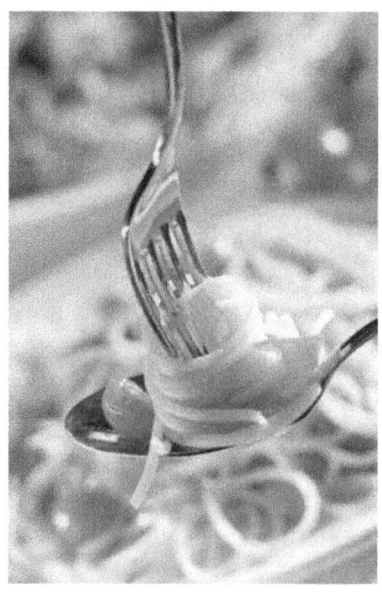

Add some zest to pasta with this delicious pressure cooker tomato sauce. Canned tomatoes increase the convenience.

Ingredients:
- 3 garlic cloves (peeled and minced)
- 1 cup carrots (peeled and diced)
- 1 cup yellow onion (diced)
- 1/4 teaspoon salt
- 1/4 teaspoon oregano (dried)

- 1 can crushed tomatoes (28 oz. can)
- 1 1/2 tablespoons olive oil
- 1/2 teaspoon parsley (dried)
- 1/2 teaspoon basil (dried)
- 1 lb. fettuccine noodles
- Salt and pepper to taste

Directions:

Heat olive oil in a pressure cooker over medium heat. Add onion and 1/4 teaspoon salt. Stir until onions are clear. Stir in remaining ingredients. Add lid and bring to pressure. Cook 40 minutes. On stovetop, cook fettuccine according to package directions. Depressurize cooker and remove lid. Stir. Add salt and pepper as desired. Put sauce in bowl to use with fettuccine.

Serves: 4

# Tender & Tasty Chicken and Rice

The pressure cooker method delivers flavorful, tender rice, chicken, and veggies in this easy to prepare meal.

Ingredients:
- 3 garlic cloves (peeled and minced)
- 4 skinless, boneless chicken breasts (approximately 3 oz. each)
- 1/2 cup carrots (peeled and chopped)
- 1/2 teaspoon salt
- 1 tablespoon vegetable oil
- 2 cups chicken broth
- 1 cup frozen peas
- 1/4 cup celery (chopped)
- 1 1/2 cups long grain white rice
- Salt and pepper to taste

Directions:

Heat oil in pressure cooker over medium-high heat. Brown the chicken on each side and remove from cooker. Add vegetables and 1/2 teaspoon salt. Cook 5 minutes, stirring occasionally. Stir in remaining ingredients and put chicken on top. Lock lid and bring cooker to high pressure over medium-high heat. Reduce heat to medium low. Cook 15 minutes. Use quick release method. Open cooker and remove chicken. Fluff rice before serving.

Serves: 4

# Quick & Easy Pressure Cooker Chili

Soak beans the night before to enjoy a delicious bowl of chili that is ready in no time. Garnish with cheddar cheese before serving for extra appeal.

Ingredients:
- 1/2 cup red onion (peeled and chopped)
- 1 1/2 cups dried kidney beans (presoaked and drained)
- 1 1/2 cups dried black beans (presoaked and drained)
- 4 garlic cloves (peeled and chopped)
- 1 teaspoon salt
- 3 tablespoons vegetable oil
- 2 tablespoons chili powder
- 1 cup red bell pepper (deseeded, cored and diced)
- 1 tablespoon tomato paste
- 1 tablespoon ground cumin
- 2 1/2 cups water

- 1 can yellow corn (15 oz. can)
- 1 can crushed tomatoes (14- 1/2 oz. can)

Directions:

Heat oil in pressure cooker over medium-high heat. Add onion, garlic, 1 teaspoon salt, and bell pepper. Cook 5 minutes, stirring occasionally. Stir in dry seasonings and tomato paste. Cook for 2 minutes. Add in remaining ingredients except for corn. Stir. Lock lid in place and bring to high pressure. Reduce heat to medium. Cook 30 minutes. Remove from heat, letting pressure release naturally for 15 minutes. Quick release remaining pressure and remove lid. Stir in corn and let sit 3 minutes.

Serves: 6

# Tilapia with Basil Tomato Sauce

This tasty dish will be a hit with its delightfully different basil tomato sauce.

Ingredients:
- 4 tilapia fillets (6 oz. each)
- 2 tablespoons olive oil
- 1/4 cup onion (minced)
- 1 teaspoon basil (dried)
- 1/4 teaspoon thyme (dried)
- 1 can crushed tomatoes (16 oz. can)
- 1 teaspoon salt

Directions:

Heat oil in pressure cooker over medium heat. Add onions and cook until translucent. Add fillets and cook two minutes. Add remaining ingredients. Lock lid and bring to high pressure. Reduce heat to medium. Cook 5 minutes. Quick release and remove lid. Serve with cornbread and salad.

Serves: 4

## Seasonal Vegetable Stew

You'll be pleased with the results of this delicious vegetable stew. It is a creative way to use the colorful yellow and green zucchini from your garden.

Ingredients:
- 1/2 cup onion (chopped)
- 1/2 cup red bell pepper (deseeded, cored, and sliced)
- 4 cups zucchini (sliced)
- 3 tablespoons olive oil
- 2 garlic cloves (peeled and minced)
- 1 teaspoon salt
- 1 can diced tomatoes (15 oz. can)
- 1/2 teaspoon pepper
- 1/2 cup carrots (peeled and thinly sliced)
- 1/4 cup celery (diced)
- 1 teaspoon oregano (dried)
- 1 teaspoon dried basil (dried)

Directions:

Heat oil in pressure cooker over medium-high heat. Stir in bell pepper, garlic, and onion. Cook 5 minutes. Add remaining ingredients. Cook 2 minutes, stirring once. Lock lid and bring cooker to high pressure over high heat. Reduce heat to medium and cook 5 minutes. Let pressure release naturally.

Serves: 4

# Too Good to Miss Chicken N Dumplings

Quick and delicious, this meal will likely become one of your favorites.

Ingredients:
- 1/4 cup onion (diced)
- 1/2 cup celery (diced)
- 2 lbs. boneless, skinless chicken breasts (diced)
- 1 cup chicken stock
- 1 teaspoon black pepper
- 2 teaspoons salt
- 1/4 teaspoon thyme (dried)
- 1 tablespoon baking powder
- 2 eggs
- 2/3 cup milk
- 2 cups flour

Directions:

Put vegetables, herbs, stock, 1 teaspoon salt, pepper, and chicken in pressure cooker. Lock lid and cook at low pressure 15 minutes. Do a quick release and remove chicken. Wrap it in foil.

Add eggs, salt, baking powder, and remaining salt to a medium bowl. Whisk until mixture bubbles. Add 1 cup flour, whisking to combine. Use a large spoon to combine remaining flour.

Bring liquid in cooker to a boil. Use a tablespoon to measure and drop dough "dumplings" into pressure cooker. Lock lid and bring to high pressure over high heat. Reduce heat to medium. Cook 5 minutes. Remove from heat; quick release pressure. Shred chicken and stir in with dumplings. Add salt and pepper to taste.

Serves: 6

# So Simple Vegetarian Baked Beans

Although this recipe is a bit longer than a 30 minute cooking time, it's too good not to include. It's hard to believe these delicious baked beans didn't bake for hours in the oven. The trick is soaking the beans overnight.

Ingredients:
- 2 cups navy beans (soaked overnight)
- 1/4 cup white or yellow onion (minced)
- 1 teaspoon pepper
- 1 teaspoon dry mustard
- 1/4 cup catsup
- 1/4 cup molasses
- 1/3 cup brown sugar
- Salt to taste
- 3 1/2 cups water

Directions:

Put all the ingredients with the exception of the salt into the pressure cooker. Lock the lid and bring to pressure over high heat. Reduce heat to medium and cook 45 minutes. Let pressure escape naturally. Remove lid and stir. Add salt to taste.

Serves: 6

# Scrumptious Sweet Potatoes and Pork

Bright orange sweet potatoes make a delicious side dish to this alternative to red meat.

Ingredients:
- 2 cups sweet potatoes (peeled and chopped)
- 1/4 cup onion (peeled and sliced into rings)
- 2 cups russet or white potatoes (peeled and chopped)
- 2 lbs. pork (cut into 8 pieces)
- 1/2 cup water
- 1 teaspoon thyme
- 1/2 teaspoon sage
- 2 tablespoons catsup
- 1/4 teaspoon pepper
- 2 tablespoons brown sugar

Directions:

Brown the meat in a medium skillet. Place in pressure cooker with onions and potatoes. Add brown sugar, spices, catsup, and water. Put lid on pressure cooker. Bring to high pressure over high heat. Reduce heat to medium. Cook for 10 minutes. Remove pot from heat and release the pressure.

Serves: 4-6

# Spur of the Moment Swiss Steak

This popular dish is easy to make for a special occasion or a regular weekday meal. Fresh vegetables from the store or garden add extra taste and appeal.

Ingredients:
- 2 cups carrots (cut into large chunks)
- 2 lbs. round steak (cut into 2-inch squares)
- 2 teaspoons olive oil
- Salt and pepper to taste
- 1/4 teaspoon garlic powder
- 1/2 cup onion (chopped)
- 2 cups potatoes (peeled and cut into large chunks)
- 2 cups water
- 3 cups beef broth
- 1 can tomato paste (6 oz. can)

Directions:

Dust meat with garlic powder and pepper. Add oil to pressure cooker. Brown both sides of meat and remove. Add onions and brown. Return meat to cooker with potatoes and carrots on top. Add tomato paste, water, and beef broth. Put the lid on the cooker and bring to high pressure. Reduce heat to medium and cook 10 minutes. Remove from heat and let pressure drop naturally.

Serves: 5

# Queen of Crab

This winner recipe is queen for crab foodie. The delicious crab on melted butter makes it one of the favorite to have on special day. Any quantity of it will not be sufficient enough!!

**Prep Time:** 3 min.
**Serving Size:** 12

Ingredients:
- **Crab Legs, King size – 64 oz.**
- **Melted butter - 1/4 cup**
- **Water - 1 cup**
- **Lemon wedges - 3**

Directions:
1. At first take the crab legs; make half pieces of them.
2. Then take your electric cooker and place its inner pot. Add in crab legs and water in the given inner pot.
3. Now close the lid on top of the Electric cooker, lock it and then close the valve for pressure release. Press the button given for making vegetable or fish food.

Then set out cooker timer at 4 min. Let the timer reach out to zero.
4. Then open the valve to release the entire pressure. After all the steam gets released, take off the lid. Enjoy with lemon wedges and melted butter.

# Lobster Sea Mania

Another sea food preparation but it includes lobster, which is quick to prepare and more importantly gives hassle free cooking experience. Great one for sea food beginners!!

**Prep Time:** 5 min.
**Serving Size:** 12

Ingredients:
- Lobsters - 5 pieces of 16 oz. Each
- Melted butter for dipping - 1/4 cup
- White wine - 1/2 cup
- Water - 1 cup

Directions:
1. At first take your electric cooker and place its inner pot. Add in wine, lobster and wine in the given inner pot.
2. Now close the lid on top of the Electric cooker, lock it and then close the valve for pressure release. Press

the button given to make vegetable or fish recipes. Then set the time of the cooker at 5 min. Let the timer reach out to zero.
3. Then open the valve to release the entire pressure. After all the steam gets released, take off the lid. Enjoy it with dipping of melted butter.

# Frozen Paste Chicken

Chicken & pasta dishes are easy one but has the potential to compete with finest of pasta cuisines. This chicken recipe is somewhat different from other chicken dishes and surely deserves to be try-out at least once.

**Prep Time:** 20 min.
**Serving Size:** 4

Ingredients:
- Tomato sauce - 24 oz.
- Your choice of favorite pasta - 8 oz.
- Pepper and sea salt as required
- Chicken breasts, frozen – 4 breasts
- Bay leaf - 1
- Chopped basil (optional)

Directions:
1. At first take your electric cooker and place its inner pot. Add in all of the mentioned ingredients in the given inner pot.

2. Now close the lid on top of the Electric cooker, lock it and then close the valve for pressure release. Press the button given to make soup or stew. Now set out the cooker's timer at 20 min. Let the timer reach out to zero.
3. Then open the valve to release the entire pressure. After all the steam gets released, take off the lid. Garnish the dish with cheese and basil. Enjoy!!

# Conclusion

Pressure cooking is one of the best choices you'll have when cooking for your family. Like fast food, it will be a fast meal option that can feed your family. However, pressure cooking doesn't include all the fat, cholesterol and calories that are found in the food of most fast food franchises. You'll also know everything that your family is eating in each dish, which should give you some peace of mind.

Just because you are pressure cooking, doesn't mean you'll have to sacrifice taste. There are plenty of delicious meals that are chock-full of flavor that can be prepared in a pressure cooker in as little as 30 minutes. The only limitation you'll face is your imagination when you learn how to cook with a pressure cooker.

You'll also be able to prepare lean, heart healthy meals with the pressure cooker. Food can directly impact the health of your body and you'll want to do all you can to ensure you are living a healthy lifestyle when possible. With a pressure cooker, you can do all of that and ensure that the health of your family is properly maintained.

Thank you again for purchasing my Kindle book.

www.ingramcontent.com/pod-product-compliance
Lightning Source LLC
Chambersburg PA
CBHW071438070526
44578CB00001B/126